Eliminate Your Debt An In Depth Guide

Dean Foster

Published by Alan Newton, 2023.

While every precaution has been taken in the preparation of this book, the publisher assumes no responsibility for errors or omissions, or for damages resulting from the use of the information contained herein.

ELIMINATE YOUR DEBT AN IN DEPTH GUIDE

First edition. April 11, 2023.

Copyright © 2023 Dean Foster.

ISBN: 979-8215648339

Written by Dean Foster.

Introduction

Money is a sensitive matter to plenty of people. In a lot of households, talking about money among family is still incredibly taboo. Much like it is with topics of sex, politics, or even religion, most people just tend to be very sensitive when it comes to talking about their financial philosophies. Perhaps, this is partly to blame as to why so many people find themselves in financial ruin right now. There are all sorts of global issues that surround money and finance such as poverty, income inequality, wage gaps, and the like. Obviously, the only real way to address these problems would be for people to start being comfortable with talking about money. A lot of it stems from the fact that people just tend to have a very poor relationship with their finances overall. This poor relationship can lead to the practice of poor financial habits that definitely won't bode well for them in the future.

While there are many forms of financial problems that are continuously troubling the world at the moment, this book is going to focus more on grassroots financial issues. In particular, this book will be taking a deep dive into the increasing debt problem among individuals in the United States. If you are reading this book with a vested interest, it might be safe to assume that you are currently in debt and you're trying to get out of it. It could also mean that you're not in debt and you're doing whatever you can to make sure that you don't get into debt in the first place. Whatever the case, the knowledge that will be highlighted in this book will be sure to help you out in stabilizing your finances. Financial security is something that everyone should be aiming for regardless of income brackets or social backgrounds. There are very few things in this life that feel as good as going to sleep at night knowing that you're financially secure for the next ten, twenty, or thirty years and on.

In order to be truly financially secure and independent, you have to make sure that you aren't living paycheck to paycheck and that you are amassing a sizable savings fund. However, that is very difficult to do when you're paying off debt. It might seem like a huge bulk of the money that you earn every month just goes to paying off any accrued debts that you might have. Then, whatever cash is left behind goes to sustaining yourself and your monthly expenses. This means that there is very little money left behind for padding your savings account. First of all, no need to worry just yet. Panicking in a situation like this is not going to do you any good. If this is similar to what your daily life is like, the very first thing that you need to do is develop a game plan. The ultimate goal here is to secure financial freedom and independence. In order to do that, you have to develop a system for yourself to eliminate your debt. This is exactly what this book is going to try to help you out with.

Make no mistake about it. There is a very real and very serious debt crisis going on. According to an article published by Lexington Law in 2020, the Federal Reserve reported the total consumer debt within the United States reached just under $4.2 trillion in late 2019. Additionally, the average American citizen owes around 10% of their disposable income to paying off car loans, credit card debts, and student loans. This doesn't even include the amount that is dedicated to paying off mortgages. In that same article, it was mentioned that the average American income has been on a steady increase since 2013. However, in spite of the increase in income, American consumers have also been increasing their debts and loans throughout that span.

It might not make sense, right? If people are earning more money, why is it that they're borrowing more money too? Well, the answer is rather simple. It's all about psychology. A lot of people mistakenly think that fiscal responsibility is mostly about the pluses and minuses in a balance sheet. However, that's not necessarily the case. This is evidenced by the fact that people are putting more money into their pockets and are still losing it at alarming rates. It's more about human psychology and the lack of understanding of basic principles surrounding financial management. Even simple concepts like lifestyle inflation, emergency funds, and asset allocations are not ideas that the general public is familiar with. This has led to the poor financial habits and practices of people all around the country. It's not enough that you're putting more money into your pocket every month. It's more important that you know how to make use of the limited financial resources that you're receiving. Unfortunately, common knowledge when it comes to financial responsibility isn't as common as you would think.

To make things clear and to set expectations properly, this book is going to focus more on personal or consumer debt. This means that the debt problem that is being discussed here pertains to the debts of individual consumers as opposed to corporations or government entities. According to an article published on Statista.com, general consumer debt composes 76% of the GDP of the United States (Szmigiera, 2019). This means that the U.S. economy is drastically growing on the backs of heavy interest rates and fees accrued from loans. Imagine how much money is going out of your pocket as a result of penalties or interest rates from the loans that you make. Collectively, these fees are powering an entire economy. However, the beneficiaries of this economic boost are not regular everyday individuals like you.

The people who most benefit from these surging interest rates and penalties are banks, loan sharks, and other financial institutions.

Let's paint a clearer picture of what the total debt ecosystem in the United States looks like. Based on a research study published on Experian.com, the total consumer debt of the United States reached a record-high in 2019 (Stolba, 2020). In fact, the study said that overall consumer debt has grown by as much as 19% since 2009, the year that marked the end of The Great Recession. Here is a list of the highest forms of consumer debt ranked from highest to lowest together with their corresponding worth:

- Mortgage Loans: $9.6 trillion (all-time high)
- Student Loans: $1.4 trillion (all-time high)
- Auto Loans: $1.3 trillion (all-time high)
- Credit Card Debt: $829 billion (all-time high)
- Home Equity Lines of Credit (HELOCs): $420 billion (all-time high)
- Personal Loans: $305 billion
- Retail Credit Card Debt: $90 billion (all-time high)

Obviously, when you look at Mortgage, Student, and Auto loans, you really know that the numbers are significant when they reach the trillion mark. However, the numbers depicted in the other forms of debt are not insignificant either. What these statistics tell us is that a huge bulk of Americans are spending a significant portion of their money on mortgages, student loans, and auto loans. Additionally, what these numbers tell us is that Americans are also spending a lot of their income on all sorts of debt-related expenses as well. However, these numbers don't tell the whole story. This boost in debt numbers can also be attributed to the fact that the American population has increased by almost 25 million people from 2009 to 2019. Naturally, as the population grows, this will translate to more people engaging in loans and debts.

While the situation might seem dire, it's not completely hopeless. The overall debt values may have increased since 2009, but statistics have shown that the average total debt for each American has decreased since then. This can mostly be attributed to the fact that the American economy has stabilized since the Great Recession and that the average income for Americans has also increased within that span. In 2009, the average annual income for Americans was $38,213. This number has increased dramatically to $50,413 in 2018. Conversely, the average total debt for Americans has decreased from $94,442 in 2009 to $90,460. So, this should serve as good news, right? Well, yes. However, it still doesn't take away from the fact that Americans are facing a very big debt crisis at the moment. Just because things might be looking up doesn't mean that there is little or no more work left to be done.

One of the most problematic parts about accruing debt is that the hole you find yourself in gets deeper and deeper the longer it takes you to solve it. If you aren't able to address your debts promptly, then interest rates and penalties are going to make a significant dent on your overall earnings. According to an article by CNBC, it's going to take more than a year for most Americans to pay off credit card debt (Leonhardt, 208). If you take a look at the statistics that were previously listed, credit card debt is ranked as the fourth highest form of debt. This means that if credit card debt is taking so long for the average consumer to address, then it's likely that the other more difficult forms of debt are lagging behind too.

If you are someone who is struggling with your debt, take the time to sit down and calculate how long it's going to take you to pay everything off. Take all of your debts into consideration here and pit them against the amount of money that you're earning. Of course, you can adjust the numbers over time assuming that you have a steady job that allows for raises and promotions. However, try to be really conservative and realistic with your estimates. Now, once you've done that, it might feel like you're in a really disheartening situation. It's okay to feel bad. No one should ever have to enjoy the feeling of paying off debts for decades. That's what you call financial insecurity; wherein the state of your finances don't make you feel comfortable or happy. Ultimately, the goal is for you to achieve financial security. This is exactly what this book is going to try to help you out with.

However, there's just no sugarcoating it. Achieving financial security and independence is going to require a lot of discipline and hard work on your part. This is not something that just happens by accident. Sure, there are some people out there who experience big breaks and get lucky with their finances. Keep in mind that these success stories from those kinds of individuals are exceptions to the rule. The rule is that you always need to work hard and stay disciplined. Yes, life may not be handing you the best of cards. You may not necessarily be a person of privilege and your big break may not come. Regardless, that is not an excuse for you not to try. At the very least, you owe it to yourself to try to achieve financial independence.

As bleak as the situation might seem, it's always important that you remind yourself that there is something that you can do about it. Of course, you might not necessarily know HOW just yet and that's why you're consulting books like these. That's a good thing. It means you're hungry to learn. It means you're eager to make a change in your life to improve your situation. It means that you have the motivation to go after what you want. That's always the first step: developing the resolve to pursue a life greater than the one you already have. So, before we start discussing the principles of you getting out of debt and achieving financial freedom, it might be a good idea for you to get to know the author of this book.

About the Author

Dean Foster works as an investment consultant who has been active in the industry for more than two decades. Throughout his career, he has worked with an array of clients, helping them all achieve and even surpass their financial goals. He understands that every case is always going to be different and he takes that into consideration when developing strategies to help his clients out. However, over the years, he has also come to find that there are certain patterns and consistencies in the narratives of the lives of his clients.

From this, Foster had a realization that perhaps people with money problems were practically committing the same mistakes that led them to where they were. He found that a lot of his clients were all experiencing and doing the same things. Naturally, when presented with the overwhelming evidence provided with the many people he has worked with over the years, Foster came to the conclusion that these *cases* were not isolated at all. Being the passionate and motivated individual that he is, Foster decided to publish *Eliminate Your Debt* in order to cascade his message to a wider and larger audience.

This book is essentially an accumulation of all of the knowledge and principles that have helped encompass Foster's career since he first started out. With it, you will be exposed to ideas that you might already be familiar with and principles that might be completely alien to you. You are going to read about things that you may already be doing in your life and things that you're going to have to start incorporating into your daily routine. Ultimately, the objective of this book is to help its readers to achieve financial security and independence. Again, there are very few things in the world that feel as good as going to sleep at night knowing that you're set for the next ten, twenty, or thirty years. That kind of feeling isn't an impossible one to chase. It's right there within your reach. You just have to have the know-how and the determination to take what you believe you are deserving of.

Chapter 1: Why You are Stuck in a Debt Rut

You can't fix a problem until you admit that there is one. Unfortunately, this is the case for a lot of people who are facing some very serious debt problems. Again, the first key to you getting out of a problem is acknowledging that you have one to begin with. So, this is precisely why this chapter is going to seek to address that problem before anything else. You must first admit to yourself that you have a problem. Then, you have to identify the reasons why you are in such a problem in the first place. Typically, this should be something that you would be able to do on your own without the aid of a book. However, there are just some people who lack the introspection that is needed to acknowledge the existence of such problems.

It's like when an alcoholic doesn't realize that they're drinking too much. They aren't able to address their alcoholism because they don't see it as a problem to begin with. Not to say that financial issues are the same as having an alcohol addiction. That's not the point here. The point is that sometimes, you can get so enveloped and engrossed in the problem that you're facing that you don't even see it as a problem anymore. You just begin to perceive it as a natural aspect of your life. That's the absolute worst position you could ever put yourself in with regards to your finances. Ignorance of the problem only exasperates it even further.

Also, consider this first chapter to be the initial phase of reverse-engineering the situation that you are in. Once you realize that you have a debt problem, you develop a resolve to achieve financial freedom and security. In order to do that, you have to reverse-engineer the process by going back to the roots of the problem to begin with. You have to understand why you fell into the problem in the first place. The reason that this is necessary is because it grants you a better perspective of your situation. When you have a more holistic view of the matter, it puts you in a better position to attack the roots of the problem directly.

Developing your *"get out of debt"* strategy is dependent on you developing a profound understanding of the situation that you're in. Keep in mind that while the principles listed here are likely to be universal in nature, it's still you who knows your situation the best. You're still the one who is going to have to develop a game plan for yourself with the guidance of the ideas that will be highlighted in this book. So, this is why you need to take the time to sit down and just think about all of the factors that could have contributed to your current condition. This way, you won't be going into the battle for financial security blindly. You would get a complete picture of the situation that you're in and you won't be blindsided or neglecting anything. As they say, it's important that you have all bases covered.

The Debt Cycle

There is a reason why so many people continuously fall into debt even though they see other individuals in their lives already struggling with debts themselves. Isn't that a weird thought to entertain? You would think that if you see something that is causing so much misery and anguish on the lives of others, you would try to avoid it for yourself. It's like when you have someone close to you who might contract a deadly disease as a result of constant cigarette smoking. You know that cigarette smoking is bad for you and so you would want to protect yourself by avoiding it at all costs. Yet, there are still some people who do not let the facts and figures deter them. Some people will continue to smoke even though they see people who suffer and even potentially die from smoking all the time. It's the same with debt. Some people might see that getting into debt is dangerous, but they still engage in it for a number of reasons either by necessity or not.

Again, debts aren't all about pluses and minuses. Psychology has a lot to do with it. The reason that so many people get into debt is because they allow their brains to trick them into thinking that the pros outweigh the cons. Unfortunately, this kind of thinking has led to the financial ruin of so many individuals. The only way to combat this mindset is to develop more mindfulness on how the brain reacts to the prospect of debt. The more control you have over your mind, the more disciplined you will be in dealing with your finances. So, it's important for you to understand why people fall into what is called the *debt cycle* in the first place.

It's true that there is some significant upside to accruing debt. It can come in handy when you're trying to invest in the future, but aren't necessarily liquid enough to do so in the moment. If the debt works out for you, then that's good. You end up building your net worth as a result of you taking a risk and accruing debt. Although, the reality for a lot of people is that most of these debts go unpaid (for a variety of reasons) over an extended period of time. As a result, they find themselves in the debt cycle and this is not a place that most people will easily be able to escape.

To put it simply, the debt cycle is the continuous accumulation of debts that lead to increased payables and expenses. Eventually, these costs get to a point wherein they are too high to overcome and the debt is then defaulted. A default is when a debtor reaches a point of failure to repay a debt including any accrued penalties and interest fees.

Here is an example of how someone might fall into a debt cycle:

Stephanie is a fresh graduate from university and has secured a job for herself at an exciting start-up company with lots of potential. She still has a lot of student loans that she has to pay for. However, with her current salary and her potential for earning more in the future within this company, she knows that she would be able to pay off her student loans in a span of 10 years. She is confident that this debt won't really deprive her of living the life that she wants because she has a great job that will help sustain her.

Over time, she makes regular payments for her student loans and she's doing so easily. On top of that, she's also doing a lot better at her job and within two years, she's successfully climbed many rungs in the corporate ladder. Stephanie has been promoted numerous times in a booming company and has been compensated fairly for her work. Stephanie is now in a position to increase her payments to pay off her debt every month because of her higher salary. If she does this, she would be able to pay off her student loans at a quicker rate and would lessen the impact of interest penalties. However, she also notices that she gets stressed out a lot on her long commute to work these days. She lives in a small and cramped apartment that is too far away from her place of work. So, now that she is earning more, she decides to take out a loan to buy a nice apartment near her place of work. She just barely has enough in her savings to afford the downpayment. However, she needs to take a loan from the bank in order for her to pay off the apartment in full. It might cost her more money, but she's able to afford it because she is earning more money now. Also, she has been told that investing in real estate is a smart use of money. By her calculations, she would also be able to pay off the apartment at around the same time she finishes paying off her student loans. So, Stephanie pulls the trigger and she buys the apartment.

Now, Stephanie is living the dream. She has a great job and is living in a nice apartment. She's still able to make regular payments to pay off her student loans and her apartment. On top of that, she's still able to set aside some money every month for her savings and occasional splurges and luxuries. Everything is going very well for her until disaster strikes. It's been found out that the company that she's working for has been taking drastic hits in the stock market and it isn't doing well sales-wise. The upper management decides that in an effort to cut costs and stop the bleeding, it has to let go of some of its senior employees who have high salaries. Stephanie happens to be one of those people.

Currently, Stephanie finds herself with her back against the wall. She still has lots of debt that she needs to pay off, but she doesn't have any source of income. Yes, she still has some emergency savings to help her get by. However, these are only going to last her for a few months. She knows that she needs to develop a game plan for herself. Her first instinct is to look for a new job elsewhere. However, no other company is willing to pay her the kind of salary that she's used to. She knows that in order for her to pay her student and mortgage loans on time, she has to maintain the same kind of salary as before. So, instead of working for another company, Stephanie decides to set up shop for herself wherein she's the boss and she gets to decide how much she earns.

Unfortunately, Stephanie doesn't have enough funds in her account to bootstrap the company herself. She also doesn't want to dip into her emergency savings unless she absolutely has to. So, in order for her to start a company, she has to take out another loan from the bank in order to gain the capital that she needs to form her team. The bank approves her loan and she is now indebted to three different entities. She's paying off three different debts at the same time. Stephanie doesn't waste any time in trying to get her company up and running. She's the boss so she's paying herself generously and she's excited to build the company from the ground-up.

The company manages to stay afloat for a few months, but things aren't really picking up. The company is just bleeding too much cash, most of it going to salary expenses. Now, Stephanie has a choice that she has to make. One option is that she allows her company to die an early death so that she can maintain her salary and make regular payments for her loans. The other option is that she lowers her salary in order for her company to live. However, this also means that she suffers penalties as a result of her not being able to make her payments on time. Thinking long-term, Stephanie decides that she will cut her salary so that her company has a shot at surviving and eventually growing in the future.

In order to compensate for her salary cut, Stephanie has to resort to borrowing from friends and family to make sure that she is still able to make regular payments to the bank. As a result, Stephanie accrues even more debt for herself from other sources. Stephanie is now caught in a cycle of having to take on more debt in an effort to pay off other debts. Before she knows it, things begin to spiral out of control and she finds herself stuck under a mountain of debt that she doesn't know how to pay off any longer. She's stuck in the debt cycle and she doesn't know how to get out of it.

Breaking Out of the Debt Cycle

Breaking out of the debt cycle is no easy task. This is especially true for people who are unaware of how deep they are into the problem. However, it's not totally impossible either. There is a way out for everyone as you will find out later in this book. However, before we get there, it's important that you first sit with your situation and familiarize yourself with all of the variables. You might already be eager to know about how you can escape the debt cycle. Don't worry. You'll get there. For now, there are still various concepts and ideas that you need to acquaint yourself with. This way, you will have all of the necessary tools to help you improve your financial situation.

Living on Borrowed Money

In order for you to be truly financially secure and independent, you have to be able to set your priorities straight. Whatever money that you have in your possession should be considered as a scarce resource. You only have so much money to devote to certain things in your life. So, with that, you have to learn how to prioritize spending the money that you have. In addition to that, you also have to make sure that you are disciplined in how you spend the money that you DON'T have. It's very important that you put an emphasis on the latter because many people are guilty of living on borrowed money.

One of the main reasons that people eventually find themselves in a state of financial ruin is that they recklessly live life on borrowed money. If you ever get to have money in your possession that you attain from borrowing, you have to consider that cash as money that you don't have. It's borrowed. It's not yours. If you have the opposite kind of mindset, it can be very easy to just recklessly spend that cash (which isn't yours) on things that you don't really need. Thus, you end up racking up a significant amount of debt on non-essential items.

Ultimately, there is just one single principle that you need to follow in order for you to stay out of debt. Any purchase that you make should be done with cash that comes out of your own pocket. Of course, there will be instances wherein this will be impossible. However, if you really want to stay on top of your cash, then you need to be as disciplined as you can possibly be. If you are just consistently paying cash outright with every purchase that you make, you are effectively preventing yourself from incurring any debt. This isn't a mindset that is merely reserved for people who don't have any debts to speak of. On the contrary, this is a mindset that is even more important for people who are living with huge piles of debt. It's going to be a lot easier for you to get out of debt when you're not adding on to it consistently.

Don't try to downplay this issue either. A critical mass of people who are in debt got to where they are as the result of living in borrowed money. These kinds of habits can only fuel a person's likelihood to remain stuck in a debt cycle. Credit card debt, in particular, has risen to some very alarming rates in the United States. Unfortunately, it's not always possible for people to get loans these days, especially when the market is stuck in a particularly fragile time. So, where do people turn to for instant spending power when they don't have the cash? Credit cards. If you happen to be a credit card owner, be very careful with the relationship that you have with that device. It has a tendency to lull you into a false sense of financial security. When you are using your credit card to pay for everything, you are essentially living on borrowed money. Credit cards make it so much more accessible for you to make use of money that isn't even yours to begin with.

It happens all too often. You might see a nice pair of boots in the store window and you immediately fall in love with it. You walk into the store and ask about its price. When you look at the price tag, it puts you off to the idea of buying it after all. You know that you don't have the cash on-hand to buy it. However, what you do have is a credit card. Also, your mind is practically set on buying the boots. It was wired that way the moment you first laid eyes on it. So, you try to trick yourself into believing that you can actually afford the boots. The presence of your credit card makes it even easier for you to do so. After all, you tell yourself that you're eventually going to find the money to pay these boots off before the credit card bill comes. So, what do you do? You end up swiping your card and spending money that you don't have for something you don't even really need.

If this happens just once or twice, then maybe you can get away with it. However, again, it lulls you into a false sense of security thinking that you're eventually going to be able to pay for anything that you buy. Before you know it, you're doing it too often to the point that your income just isn't able to sustain yourself anymore. Credit cards can be very dangerous, especially for new credit card owners. Just because you have a new credit card doesn't mean that you can get free money whenever you want. That's just not how it works. Heck, even the more experienced credit card users are susceptible to making some crucial financial mistakes as well.

Credit Cards Offer Increased Temptations of Spending Beyond Your Means

Again, the basic idea of living on borrowed money is built on spending cash that isn't even yours. You have to adopt a mindset wherein you can only buy things with money that you have on hand. Otherwise, you fall into the trap of spending unearned money. This is also called spending beyond your means. A lot of people seem to think that it's easier to just try to find more money to pay off incurred credit card debts. However, the truth is that it's just a lot easier to avoid using credit cards to spend unearned money altogether.

Interest Rates are Silent Killers

Another dangerous component of credit card payments is the concept of installments. A lot of the time, people will not be able to make certain purchases in terms of one-time payments. For example, a high-end television set might cost $1200. In a single purchase, $1200 can be very painful on the wallet. However, when you're afforded an opportunity to stagger your payments over the course of one year in 12 installments, then it makes you feel like it isn't as big as a blow on your bank account. This might be true if these staggered payments don't have any interest fees attached to them. However, a lot of the time, a one-time $1200 purchase can turn into $1500 staggered over the course of a year. So, you effectively end up paying more money than necessary with borrowed cash.

Credit Card Transactions are Instant Debts

Whether you have the money to pay them off or not, credit card transactions are instant debts. They make it so easy for you to get into debt and to keep you in debt for an extended period. Of course, this might not be an issue for people who are able to make timely payments for their credit card bills every month. However, for those who are already in the red with their finances, credit cards just have a tendency to make things worse. While other people might see credit cards as a luxurious convenience, they are also known to exacerbate the problem significantly.

Spending Borrowed Money Makes it More Difficult to Keep Track of Your Finances

Lastly, spending borrowed money through credit card transactions just makes it a lot more difficult to keep track of the state of your finances. When you only spend cash that you have on-hand, it's a lot easier to really feel the pain of that expense. You know that you're losing money right in that moment. However, at least you won't have to worry about incurring any additional charges for that transaction in the future. A credit card transaction is different. You don't lose any cash at the moment of purchase even though you're incurring even more debt. On top of that, depending on your transaction, there may be interest rates and other credit-card related fees that you might not be keeping track of at that moment.

An Ongoing Struggle with Debt Culture

Back in 2008, at the height of The Great Recession, The New York Times writer David Brooks published an article about his thoughts on the debt culture in the United States. In his article, he talked about whether who was to be blamed for the collapse of the economy during that year. Was it the fault of the *predatory lenders*, as he called them, who preyed on the vulnerability of desperate Americans who were in need of instant cash and credit lines? Rather, was it the fault of the gullible and misinformed Americans who let their financial illiteracy get the best of them?

In particular, Brooks referenced the case of one Diane McLeod, a single mother who was going through a divorce and had health complications. She was working two jobs and was barely able to make ends meet. So, she found herself succumbing to the aggressive marketing ploys of credit card companies who were eager to capitalize on her situation. Supposedly, mortgage lenders had led her to believe that her house was rising in value and that it would make for perfect collateral for a credit line. Unfortunately, it was found out that these lenders had no interest in whether or not she would be able to pay off her loans. They merely got their money back from initial lending fees and pawned off the loans to third-party lenders. Much to Diane's dismay, she found herself under a mountain of debt and in worse financial shape than she had ever been.

There are two sides of the coin here. For the defenders of capitalism, one wouldn't place the blame on the *predatory lenders* who are also just doing their parts in a free market. These are the same people who will say that Diane should have known better and that she must assume responsibility for her actions. They say that she must have understood from the very start that credited money is not the same as having spot cash. So, it was her own negligence that led to her financial ruin.

There are also those who will say that people like Diane just aren't in the right positions to be making these calls for themselves. Defenders of people like Diane will say that their circumstances and situations will cause them to make poor financial decisions under duress. They say that these lending companies and banks understand this and are absolutely ruthless in capitalizing on the situation.

Now, you can't say that one side is wrong and the other side isn't. Both sides view the issue from different perspectives and they raise some very valid points. Although, regardless of however you might choose to look at the issue, it's plain to see that there is a very serious problem here that needs to be addressed. There is a certain unhealthy culture in the United States that is further gaining prominence as the result of the financial illiteracy of the masses and the ruthless aggression of credit companies.

Although, it's not just Americans who are struggling with debt culture at the moment. It might seem totally weird just how unnatural the concept of living within one's means has become in the modern world. Perhaps, the prevalence of consumerism in mainstream media has just exacerbated the problem even more. Maybe social media culture has people shifting their priorities and chasing after things that they shouldn't be prioritizing with their money. Whatever the case, the issue of debt has transcended American financial culture. It has also managed to stay prevalent in other countries as well, especially in the Western world.

These days it's just so easy for people to gain access to money that isn't theirs. You can make the argument that it's much easier now than it has ever been to buy luxurious items like houses, cars, jewelry, watches, and designer clothes without even having to spend a single dollar. This is all made possible through readily available and accessible credit lines. Heck, these days, you don't even have to walk into a bank to avail of a credit card. Banks all over the world have set up online application forms wherein you just submit all of your necessary documents. Within a week, a credit card will show up at your doorstep and you are free to use it however you see fit (for better or for worse). Yes, there are many people all over the world who are struggling with managing their finances and fixing their debt. Obviously, these banks, credit card companies, loan sharks, lenders, and other financial predators don't care much about the fact that they're making it so easy for people to make poor financial choices. At the end of the day, they have to do whatever it takes to generate profit for themselves. Yes, there are regulations that should be put in place to mitigate the problem to a certain extent. However, the whole debt culture is still ultimately dependent on the discipline and willpower of an individual. This is exactly the reason why financial literacy and independence are so important when fighting off debt.

Chapter 2: Good Debt, Bad Debt, and Other Money Myths

A huge part of developing a good relationship with debt is understanding that there are many layers to it. There are many dimensions to debt and it would be incredibly irresponsible to just generalize debt as this or that. Truth be told, there are plenty of people who will say that debt is just a very normal and even natural part of living in the modern world. Also, these same people might also be financially well off and stable. So, if these people are able to engage in loans and debts while staying financially secure, shouldn't you be able to do the same? The short answer is yes. You can. However, it's all very complicated.

Again, this book was made in an effort to debunk all of the misinformation and myths that are circulating around out there. All of this fake information surrounding money and debt will only lead to the financial ruin of more and more people. The only way to combat the circulation of misinformation is to communicate hard truths and verifiable facts to as many people as possible. What this chapter is going to focus on is the many complicated and nuanced layers of debt. As a fiscally responsible adult, you owe it to yourself to really understand the many dimensions of debt. This is so you are better prepared to handle certain situations that concern you taking out loans in your life.

It's true when they say that debt is inescapable for a lot of people in the world. As much as possible, you would want to pay for everything that you have with your own cash that you have on hand. This is the idea of living within your means, right? We talked about this earlier in the previous chapter. However, living within your means is also a luxury that not all people have. For example, if you need to invest in a home or in college education, you might not always have the cash on hand to pay for these things. However, having a place to stay and a degree from a reputable college are vital to your financial success in the future. It wouldn't be smart for you to hold off on going to college while you save up all of the money that you need to pay for tuition. Also, as much as possible, you would never want to put yourself in a position wherein you're homeless, right? In these times, loans are necessary. In fact, one can even make the argument that taking out a loan to go to college is a smart thing to do. However, how does one exactly go about making such an argument? Well, these are the things that you're going to learn about as you make your way through this chapter.

As you make your way through life, you will find that you will be faced with various difficult choices that you have to make surrounding your finances, especially when it comes to dealing with debt. When you reach these moments, you have to know how to answer certain questions. Is this loan (and all of the interest payments you will be making to pay it off) going to be worth it in the future? Are the prospective benefits of taking out a loan going to eclipse the cons of interest fees or potential penalties? These are very important questions that could either make or break you financially. Sometimes, good debts can really pay off for you in a significant manner. They can help you to achieve financial independence and security. However, on the other side of the coin, bad debts can leave you rotting in the compost heap of your own poor financial choices. Truly, you would never want to put yourself in the position of the latter.

The objectives of this chapter all revolve around you being able to put yourself in a position to make smart choices about the kinds of debts that you engage in. You have to know when to pull the trigger, but you also have to know when to pull the plug.

Not All Debt is Created Equal

It's no secret that debt is something that keeps a lot of Americans awake at night. You might be lying in your bed, just tossing and turning as you try to think of ways to make your monthly payments on time so that you don't accrue any more penalties and fees. Literally millions of Americans are stressed and anxious about the debt that they have. Who wouldn't be? It strikes fear into the hearts of many. The rising debt problem has become so rampant and so serious for a lot of Americans. It has gotten to a point where a lot of people consider it to be something to be avoided at all costs. Somehow, debt has become demonized in the world of finance and money management. However, that shouldn't really be the case.

The very first thing that you need to understand about debt is that not all debts are created equal. There is such a thing as good debt and there is also such a thing as bad debt. Obviously, good debt is something you should feel free to engage in, while bad debt is the one that you need to avoid at all costs. The key here merely remains in you being able to identify the difference. Another factor that makes the concept of *good* and *bad* debt so complicated is the fact that it's all relative. There are certain forms of debt that are good for a specific group of people and are simultaneously bad for another group of people. It all depends on your current financial situation and the amount of risk that surrounds you.

How Do You Know if Debt is Good or Bad?

That's an excellent question. We're going to get into the specifics of different kinds of debts as we go along. However, if anything feels too confusing or complicated for you, just remember this one thing: if a debt will help increase your net worth or your future value, then it's good. If a debt doesn't add value to your life and you can't afford to pay for it, it's bad debt. That's just the general rule of thumb that you need to hold in your heart as you make your way through your financial journey. So as long as you remember that golden rule, you should turn out fine. However, that shouldn't stop us from delving a little deeper into the concept of good and bad debt.

How Do You Know if You Have Too Much Debt?

Before we get into the nitty gritty of what constitutes good or bad debts, it's also important to make an important point. It's possible for you to have too much of a good thing, even when you're talking about debts. Just because a debt is classified as *good* doesn't mean that you should partake in it. Ultimately, the answer to the question of whether you already have too much debt or not lies in your debt-income ratio.

It's going to be different for most people. However, the best practice would be for you to review your current financial state before you decide on taking in more debt. First, you need to add up all of the debt payments that you are currently making on a monthly basis. Take the sum of that computation and then divide it by your monthly income. The quotient of that equation should leave you with your debt-income ratio.

For example, let's say that your current monthly payments are as follows:

- $1,000 for student loans
- $1,000 for mortgage
- $800 for a car payment
- $300 for credit card payments and other bills

In total, you would have a monthly debt of $3,100. If you have a monthly income of $6,000, then you are in trouble. That is a debt-income ratio of 51.67% Depending on who you ask, you are going to get many different pieces of advice on this. However, you should try to shoot for a debt-income ratio of no more than 43%. With this number, it's going to be relatively easy for you to make your monthly payments and still have enough cash left over to sustain yourself and add to your savings. Also, a lot of the time, lenders will not be willing to fork over any more cash for you to use on good investments if your debt-income ratio is too high. Let's say it would be a good investment for you to invest in quality real estate that is going to shoot up in value over the next decade. For you to get the cash to invest in that real estate, you need to take out a loan. You won't be able to do so if the lenders or banks see that you're already being crushed by all of your accumulated monthly payments.

Examples of Good Debt

Generally speaking, debt is good if it's going to end up serving you in the future. Again, as much as possible you should be paying for things with cash that you have on-hand. However, not all of us are blessed with unlimited pockets. So, we have to turn to debt every once in a while to help us pay for the things that we need now and can actually add value to our lives both in the present and the future. So as long as you know that you would be able to make monthly payments in a prompt manner, you should be willing to engage in good debts.

Good debts will afford you the ability to really manage your finances more effectively. Why would you spend all of your emergency savings on a house when you know that you can take a reasonable loan out for it? Here are a few examples of good debts that you could look into as smart investments for your future:

Student Loans

As the old cliché goes, education is one of the most important things you could ever invest your money into. A lot of people seem to buy into this idea in a literal sense. Again, the accumulated total value of student loans in the United States is at $1.4 trillion. So, obviously, there are loads of people who are investing in their education. Now, this isn't necessarily a bad thing. In fact, it's always a good idea for you to invest in your education if you know that it's going to help you gain a competitive advantage in your career.

Ultimately, the long-term goal here is for you to expand your capacity to earn money. Sometimes, depending on your line of work, you need to have undergone formal training and education in order for you to really rake in the big bucks. So, if taking out a student loan means you get more chances of winding up as the CEO of a massively successful company in the future, then it's a good debt.

Mortgages

Many experts will tell you that a mortgage is probably the best form of debt that you could possibly take. Obviously, you need a place to live in. It's a literal need. Shelter is something that is vital to your survival of a human being. If that's not worth taking out a loan for, then what is? Also, on top of that, mortgages tend to also be good investments in the long run. So, not only are you taking on debt as a way of securing shelter for yourself. You are also taking on debt to invest in something that is going to appreciate in value for the years to come.

We're not to get specific on the numbers because it really depends on where you are. However, typically the interest rates that you pay on mortgages aren't going to be as high as the appreciation values of your home. In essence, you're going to be overpaying for your home now because of the interest rates on your mortgage. However, ultimately, your home is bound to appreciate in values that will far surpass what you pay in interest rates.

Pro-tip: Experts say that you should limit your mortgage payments to no more than 36% of your gross monthly income. This way, your payments are more manageable and you don't get overloaded with debt.

Home Equity Loans

Depending on who you ask, home equity loans can be considered good or bad debt. It all really depends on the state of your financial situation and what you intend to use this loan for. So, essentially, the way that home equity loans work is that they function as mortgages. You would be able to get a loan by putting your home up as collateral. Now, typically, these home equity loans have relatively low interest rates just like mortgages. This makes them easier to pay off in the long run because they aren't as expensive as other kinds of loans. So, the money that you get from this loan can go into paying off other debts with very high interest rates like credit card debts or car payments.

In theory, this sounds like a good idea. Also, there are plenty of people who have tried this technique and have made it work to their favor. However, it's still a very big risk. Should an unforeseen circumstance materialize rendering you unable to make payments, you will have to face the realities of having your home foreclosed.

Small Business Loans

Lastly, there are small business loans. There's a certain financial security that you achieve when you work within the structure of a solid company as an employee. You get benefits and a constant stream of monthly income. You also get the prospects of raises and promotions in the future. However, you will never be earning as much money as the people who own the company. This is why some people, especially those who are entrepreneurial, would rather just invest their time and money into setting up businesses of their own.

And it's true. When you're the owner of your business, you get substantially more out of your company than your employees would. However, there is still a risk here. Not all businesses succeed. This is why you really have to do your part as an entrepreneur to ensure that the business will be profitable in the long run. Also, it's not easy securing a small business loan. You are going to have to present a solid company profile and business plan to prove to the lenders that you have what it takes to pay your loan back. Fortunately, these hoops that you have to jump through also serve as safeguards for yourself. If lenders see that you don't have what it takes to run a profitable business, then they might end up protecting you from engaging in bad debt.

Examples of Bad Debt

If it's going to take you 10 years to pay for something that won't even last you for half that amount of time, then it's a very bad investment. That's bad debt. If you see a pair of designer shoes that will take you five years to pay off in full, then just walk away. This is especially true if those shoes won't even last you that long and are not crucial to your money-earning capabilities. After two or three years, those shoes will either be broken or will be out of style. You'll still have to be paying them off because of how expensive they are. This is the whole principle of bad debt: buying something (with money that isn't yours) you don't need and won't serve you in the long run.

Generally, if something doesn't appreciate in value or if it won't earn you money in the future, then you shouldn't be taking out a loan for it. You shouldn't be taking out a loan for clothes, vacations, furniture, lavish parties, and whatnot. These are things that are either consumable (meaning they have a shelf life) or will depreciate in value once you have them. Here are a few examples of bad debts that you want to avoid as much as possible:

Car Loans

Cars are luxuries. There are no ifs, ands, or buts about it. You can argue all you want about how cars really help make your life easier and more convenient. You can even make the argument that time is money and that owning a car will help you save time. However, at the end of the day, the second that you drive a brand new car out of the dealership, you're burning more and more money by the minute. Sure, there are some cars out there that increase in value; for example, well-kept vintage cars. However, if you have enough cash to afford those kinds of cars in the first place, then you wouldn't need to be looking into the distinctions between good and bad debts.

On top of that, the expenses for a car don't stop at merely purchasing it. You're going to have to pay for gas, parking, and general maintenance as well. These add on to the money that you're paying for your car every month. Sure, you might be able to strike a good deal if you're looking into the used car market. However, for the most part, car loans are bad debts and you want to avoid them as much as possible.

Payday Loans

Payday loans are notorious in the finance community for being the worst possible kinds of loans that you could get. These kinds of loans come with incredibly outrageous interest rates. Most of the time, people resort to making payday loans when they need quick access to cash. These debts are designed to also be paid within a short amount of time. Usually, payments are made once a person's salary check comes in. Hence, the name *payday loan*.

Payday loans don't usually amount to big dollar values. Typically, they will fall just under around $500. However, the fees on these loans are so high, that it just doesn't make sense for people to resort to these kinds of transactions for quick cash. Sometimes, you might take a loan out for $500, and you could be ending up paying up to $150 in fees. That is not an insignificant amount by any stretch, especially relative to how much money you're borrowing in the first place. It might be better to incur credit card debts as opposed to payday loans. However, credit card debts aren't good either.

Credit Card Debts

Yes, the percentage rates of credit cards aren't going to be as outrageous as those of payday loans. However, these are still not smart debts to be taking on. Credit card debts are bad debts, especially when they are used for non-essential transactions. Sure, there are some instances wherein using a credit card is smart. For example, there are certain credit card companies that offer rebates, rewards, points, and whatnot. These are nice and there is nothing wrong with you availing of these promotions so long as you are able to pay your credit card in full every month.

If it gets to a point wherein you're chasing after these promotions, but find yourself incapable of making payments, then you're really missing the point. You're doing things wrong. Credit cards should only ever be used for essential items or emergency situations. For example, you might be at the grocery store and you don't have enough cash on you when you reach the counter. Although, you do know that you have enough cash in your account that you budgeted for these groceries. You just haven't withdrawn the money yet. Then, it would be wise to use a credit card for this transaction. After using the card, immediately withdraw your cash and set that aside. Consider that money good as spent. This way, you know that you're not incurring any debt. Credit cards in themselves aren't bad. In fact, plenty of rich people are able to maintain their riches in spite of using credit cards all the time. It's all just a matter of how you use them. Take note that being able to use your credit card properly can lead to you having a good credit score. However, all of this is dependent on you making good timely payments.

Be Smart About Your Choices

Just because a transaction has been classified as *good debt* in this book doesn't mean that you should be making it. Again, good debt can only ever really be considered good if it adds value to your future. If you're just engaging in *good debt* for the hell of it, then it's pointless. It becomes bad debt. For instance, if you're further along in your career and you feel like you need to get a master's degree for you to break the ceiling and make more money, then that's fine. You would be taking on debt, but you would also end up expanding your capacity to earn more money in the future. That's good debt. That's a good investment. You might not necessarily have the cash on-hand to fund a master's degree program. So, taking out a student loan as a means of financing your education shouldn't be a problem so as long as you know you will benefit from it in the future. Also, you have to know that you will be able to make payments promptly.

If you take a step back and look at the financial situation that you're in, it's important that you develop a proper strategy in attacking your debts. As much as possible, you only want debts that are good when you're looking at your financial portfolio. So, if you have bad debts, try your best to eliminate them as soon as possible. In the process, avoid taking on any additional debt (whether good or bad) if you still have any unpaid bad debts. Again, just because a debt is deemed or classified as *good* doesn't mean that you should just take it on. No matter if debt is good or bad, it's all going to come crashing down on you when you aren't able to control yourself. When you overload yourself with debt, you are never going to achieve financial security.

Debunking Myths About Money and Finances

There's something just so inherently entertaining about mythology and fantasy. This is why the art of storytelling has persisted in the human species for over millennia. There are definitely a lot of lessons to be learned from hearing these stories and myths from old lore. These parables and short stories are able to provide valuable perspective and philosophy on the many facets of life including its great beauties and hardships. However, there is also another face to myth as well. It isn't one of enlightenment or illumination. Rather, it's one of disillusionment and misinformation. Make no mistake about it, there are many myths circulating out there about debt, money, and financial management.

You might have heard in the past that paying off all of your debt will automatically equate to you achieving a perfect credit score. You might also be under the impression that lenders won't lend you money if they know that you can't pay them back. It's possible that you might even have heard that incurring any kind of debt or owning any sort of credit card is bad and should always be avoided. These are all examples of myths about debt and finance. If you truly want to become someone who is self-sustaining in a financial sense, you need to understand what makes all of this information false.

For this segment of the chapter, you will be briefed on a few of the many popular myths surrounding debt and finance along with why they are false.

Myth: It's Not a Big Deal to Skip Payments

On the contrary, it's a very big deal when you decide to skip payments. For one, it's a signal that you are struggling with paying your debts and that you are far from being financially secure. Keep in mind that any legitimate credit agreement comes with certain terms and conditions. You agree to these terms and conditions when you decide to borrow money. In those terms, you are designated proper payment schemes and schedules. Should you fail to adhere to those terms, then this fact will be reflected on your credit report. That's not good for you.

In addition, you might not even realize that in most loan agreements, your lender has the power to actually call in the loan. They might do this when they see that you're missing monthly payments. Calling in a loan means having you pay your entire debt in full all at once. A lender might do this because they see that you're missing payments and that it's unlikely you would be able to pay them their money back if they allow the debt to drag on. Naturally, this can place you in a rather vulnerable situation. Not only are you struggling with making monthly payments, but it's even more unlikely you would be able to pay your entire debt back in full all at once.

As much as possible, try to only take on debt that you know you can manage and sustain over an extended period of time. If you aren't feeling confident about your ability to pay your bills off every month, then you shouldn't be taking on that kind of debt.

Myth: Credit Cards for Retailers are a Good Idea

It's so easy to get lost in all of the promotions that come with credit cards from retailers. However, you have to know that these promotions are designed to inhibit your reason so that you are forced to make irrational and financially unsound choices. At face value, it can be really tempting to take on a credit card that offers a variety of benefits, points, and rewards. Who wouldn't want a credit card that offers interest-free financing or installment payments? You're practically spending that cash already with a purchase, right? So, why not just draw the payment out over the course of a year? Well, you have to be very careful before you get swept up into this kind of logic. Read the fine print and familiarize yourself with all of the nuances of these kinds of deals.

Sure, if you're a responsible credit card holder who makes your payments on time, then it shouldn't be a problem. Good for you. It means you're not really taking on any debt and that you're maximizing your rewards and benefits. However, what happens when a transaction goes awry and you find yourself unable to make the designated payment in the set amount of time? For example, let's say that you walk by a Rolex authorized dealer and you decide you want to treat yourself. You're just starting to find some stability with your income, but you don't have the kind of cash wherein you can just splurge on a Rolex on a whim. However, you know that you have a credit card that offers interest-free financing for 12 months. You do the calculations in your head and you are confident that you can pay off the watch in a year. So, you decide to treat yourself and you buy the Rolex.

For the first few months, everything might be going fine. However, then, in the seventh month, someone in your family gets sick and you have to shoulder their medical bills. These medical expenses take out a huge chunk of your monthly income. You do the computations and you realize that you can't make payments for your Rolex anymore and you probably won't be able to afford to pay it off within the allotted time frame. So, what happens when you can't make full payments within the year? Well, a variable annual percentage rate (APR) kicks in. This is where the interest rates will kill you. Depending on the bank, these rates can go as high as 20-25%. It won't even matter what kind of credit score you have. These are the rates that are stipulated in the terms and conditions when you signed on for the credit card. Always read the fine print.

Myth: If You Die Unexpectedly, Your Family Will Have to Take on Your Debt

There are plenty of people who seem to dread the idea of debt being inherited by their loved ones once they pass away. Well, that's not necessarily how debt works. If you die unexpectedly with any unsettled transactions, your family will not have to pay off your debts on your behalf. The way this works is that the assets that you leave behind are the ones that will take a hit. So, if you have any outstanding debts, your creditors are entitled to any assets like real estate, jewelry, savings, investments, and more. These things will be appraised and converted into monetary values to pay off your debts.

However, if you have no assets to leave behind at the moment of death, then any debts that you have will be written off. The only time wherein a living person will be responsible for debts upon your debt is if you engage in a joint debt. Should you die in with any unsettled joint debts, the surviving individual shall be accountable for the remaining joint balance.

Myth: Carrying a Balance on Your Credit Card Will Improve Your Credit Score

Your credit score is not dependent on you having a balance and paying it off every month. That's not how credit scores work. The only thing that you're achieving with this kind of system is making the credit card companies richer with your interest payments. So, you're essentially just taking more of your hard-earned cash and paying it forward to credit card companies without really having any of it affect your credit score for the better.

However, you shouldn't take that to mean that you can't use the credit card to help improve your credit score. In fact, many people use the credit card as a tool to boost their credit ratings. In order to do this, it's just a matter of you paying your balance off in full every single month. In addition to that, you can set a limit of yourself to how much you use your credit card. The higher the amount of available credit that you have every month, then the higher your credit rating is going to be.

Myth: Your Bank Won't Help You if You Can't Pay Off Your Debts

Never make the mistake of thinking that your banks don't care about whether you are able to pay your debts back or not. In fact, for the most part, banks might be very much invested in helping you make your payments. Whenever you feel like you're struggling with paying your debts, just reach out to your creditor right away. Open up to them about your situation and the kind of issues you're dealing with at the moment. Also, try to come up with a plan before opening up to them. Outline your next steps and let them see that you're eventually going to be able to pay them back. You just need them to give you more time.

You would be surprised to find out that banks might agree to put a hold on the interest fees of your payments or even reduce them on a temporary basis. They might be invested in helping get you back on your feet in the meantime so that you would be able to pay them off in the long-term. Sometimes, they might even be able to help you come up with a proper payment scheme to help make things easier for you.

Myth: Making Just Minimum Payments on Debts is Okay

Banks are never going to tell you this, but the *minimum payments* that they designate on your credit cards are only there to give you a false sense of financial safety. It benefits the banks more if you just keep on making minimum payments because it prolongs your debts. When you prolong your debts, this translates to higher interest fees for the bank. Sure, your credit rating won't be affected negatively and you won't be subjected to late fees and such. However, the soonest available opportunity you can get to pay off a debt in full, do so.

To paint a clearer picture, let's imagine that you have a credit card balance that amounts to $8,000. If you have a minimum monthly payment of $150 with an annual interest rate of 15%, it's going to take you 89 months to pay all of that off. On top of that, you're going to be paying an additional $5,265 in interest fees. Also, your banks are rarely ever going to advertise that interest rates are at 15% annually. Usually, they will try to be slick about it and say that interest rates are only 1.25% a month instead of 15% per year because it doesn't sound as intimidating. If you're content with just making minimum payments every time, then you're essentially paying $13,265 for an $8,000 loan. Now, if you do the calculations again, but this time you make it a point to pay $200 a month, the numbers change dramatically. It will only take you 56 months to pay the entire debt off and you only accumulate interest fees that amount to $3,159. That's not an insignificant amount by any stretch. However, it's significantly much smaller than the amount you're paying if you're just doing the minimum monthly payments.

If you need help with computing your credit card debt payments, there are various tools online that you can make use of. The built-in calculator at https://www.bankrate.com/calculators/credit-cards/credit-card-payoff-calculator.aspx is incredibly simple and free to use.

Myth: Student Loans Expire and Become Void After a Few Years

Now, this is a rather complicated myth to debunk because there are many legalities surrounding it. Yes, it's true that there is a statute of limitations on student debt. However, this only applies to private student loans. On federal student loans, there is no statute of limitations. Also, with the private student loans, the statute of limitations can differ depending on which state you live in.

A lot of people seem to think that a statute of limitations refers to an expiration date for student loans. It's like these loans will just instantly become null and void after a while. However, that's not how a statute of limitations work. A statute of limitations is essentially just the amount of time wherein a creditor is entitled to SUE you for repayment should you ever fail to make payments over an extended period of time. Just because you decide to stop paying your loans doesn't mean that they're eventually just going to go away and become void in the future. In fact, even if a creditor goes beyond the statute of limitations without suing you, they are still entitled to collecting the money from you. They just can't coerce you into doing so by means of arbitration.

It wouldn't be wise for you to stop paying your student loans to wait for one's statute of limitations to pass and go by. You'll only be killing your bank account even further with any interest fees you incur. Also, there's no guarantee that you will be protected by the law at all.

Myth: You are Only Accountable to Half of Joint Debt

Joint debts can be beneficial in trying to ease your financial burdens. You can use the spending power of two different people to make a single purchase. However, just because you're going into a joint debt venture with someone else doesn't mean that your liability is also split down the middle. At the end of the day, the two you will be liable for the entire amount. So, should the circumstance arise that your partner fails to make their payments, then you would be liable for that failure as well. The creditor can chase you down and hold you accountable for the full amount and not just your share.

However, it's different when you have a credit card account wherein one of you serves as the primary cardholder and the other serves as a supplementary cardholder. When that's the case, only the primary cardholder is liable to the creditors for the full amount.

Myth: Paying Off Your Debts Will Instantly Give You a Perfect Credit Score

That's just not how credit ratings work. With the way that credit reports are structured, they only supply information surrounding your credit standing and your credit history. So, this means that all of the details surrounding your habits in your credit history all come into play here. For example, data about failed payments can remain in your credit report for as long as seven years. Details about any filed bankruptcies can also stay for as long as a decade. Just because you cleanse yourself of any debts doesn't mean that you're going to achieve a pristine credit score. You're going to have to do so gradually.

Myth: All Debt is Bad and Credit Cards are the Devil's Toys

Truth be told, it can be very expensive when you're carrying a heavy balance accompanied with high interest rates on your credit card. High-interest loans are also very bad for your financial future and it can keep you from achieving any kind of financial security any time soon. So, in that sense, debt is really bad. You never want to be paying off interest rates or penalties that far surpass the amount that you had initially borrowed. Although, not all kinds of debt are going to lead to your financial ruin. In fact, there are certain smart debts that you can make that can help you achieve your financial goals. These kinds of debts have already been discussed previously. Should you ever decide to take on these kinds of debts, just make sure that you're really researching the best rates that you could possibly get. This way, you know that you're not being cheated out of a good deal.

Credit cards are not inherently bad tools either. In fact, they can work to your advantage if you just know how to use them properly. The reality is that you just have to make sure that you clear your card balance every single month. Wipe that slate clean. This way, you avoid paying any unwanted interest fees that have you spending more than you really need. Using your credit card for big purchases can be really good for you, especially when you have credit cards that have solid rewards programs. You can capitalize on these promotions to win rebates, travel points, electronics, discounts, and more. There is definitely a lot to gain when you are a responsible credit card user.

Also, the active usage of your credit card will help improve your credit rating. This is going to make it easier for you to take on responsible loans in the future such as home loans or small business loans. In fact, if these creditors see that you are a responsible and active credit card user, they might even offer you very low interest rates because they see your history of making payments on time. Credit card debt is bad and you should avoid it to the best of your abilities. However, if you know that you can wipe the slate clean and pay your credit card bill every month, you're going to do alright. Credit cards can be your friend.

Myth: Lenders Won't Give You Debt That You Can't Pay Back
Yes, lenders do their due diligence prior to making any decisions on whether or not to provide you with a loan. The biggest factor that

they take into consideration when thinking about whether to approve a loan is your gross income. However, lenders might not necessarily be taking into consideration what other expenses you might have in your life right now. For example, some lenders don't necessarily look into whether you have medical bills to pay or if you have outstanding debts or loans with relatives. Lenders might not ask about your spending habits and the kind of lifestyle that you have. There are plenty of things about your financial situation that a lender might not necessarily be familiar with. So, in essence, they might be approving a loan for you without knowing that there's no way that you're going to be able to pay them back.

In these situations, the person in the most optimal position to make the best judgment on whether or not you would be able to pay off the loan is yourself. It doesn't even matter what kind of debt you're incurring. If it's a small business loan, credit card debt, or a mortgage, you are the only one who really knows for sure whether you would be able to pay it off or not. You know the ins and outs of your budget because it's your money and no one knows your spending habits like you do. So, when you're requesting a loan, make sure that you're not biting off more than you can chew. These financial experts will do their best in studying you beforehand. However, anything they have to work with is dependent on the information and data that you supply to them.

Myth: Emergency Funds are Unnecessary When You Have Credit Cards

Credit cards are not equal to you having emergency funds or savings. Just because you have instant access to credit lines doesn't mean that you are excused from amassing a sizable emergency fund. Sure, should an emergency ever arise, you can always use your credit card to help get you by. For example, you lose your job and you need to pay your utility bills for the month. You can always use your credit card to make sure that the lights stay on. However, you have to know that by doing so, you are only adding to your liabilities and payables. You're doing so at a time when you're not really in the best financial shape because of your lack of a job.

It's going to get to a point wherein you will need to pay your credit card bills. If you don't have the cash on-hand to make those payments, then you're going to be subject to the mercy of penalties and interest fees. Just to be safe, make sure that you have around three to six months' worth of expenses in your emergency savings fund. This way, you have a safe and sizable buffer to keep you afloat whenever you are going through unexpected rough patches.

Myth: You Inherit a Person's Debt When You Marry Them/Your Joint Debts Become Separated if You Divorce

When you get married to someone, it's a wonderful thing. You promise to spend the rest of your lives together and to share everything with one another. Although, that doesn't mean that you also have to share debts. Just because the two of you get married doesn't mean that you are also liable for any outstanding debts that your spouse may have and vice-versa. Although, you need to be mindful of a few details here. Depending on where you live, if you make payments on any outstanding debts attributed to your spouse with your own income, then you might be legally required to continue those payments until they are paid in full or if you finalize a divorce. Also, we have already previously talked about how your joint debts don't become separated just because your marriage doesn't work out. Both of you are still liable to joint debts that you sign into when you're married regardless of how the marriage turns out.

Chapter 3: How Did You Get Here?

Where Has All Your Money Gone?

What exactly have you been doing wrong? Why did you allow things to get so bad? Well, for a lot of people who are in financial ruin, it's not often that it's going to be caused by a traumatic and sudden event. Sure, there are people who can just point to one moment in their life that shoved them into rough times. Maybe you might have lost your job. Perhaps, someone near and dear to you got sick and you've had to shoulder their medical expenses. Maybe you put all of your money into a bad business investment and you weren't able to recover any of it. Sure, these are some very bad things that can happen to you which might put you in a tough financial situation.

However, for the most part, it's not just one dramatic point in time that you can attribute your financial shortcomings to. Most of the time, it has to do with the kinds of habits that you employ in your everyday life. For most people, it's going to be a frog in hot water situation. If you're not familiar with that adage, it's a reference to a supposed scientific experiment on how frogs react to being submerged in hot water. There are many who say that the story is purely fabricated and there are those who will say that whether or not the story is true is irrelevant. Anyway, in the supposed experiment, the researchers had placed a frog into an empty pot. Then, they had heated water in a separate pot and brought it to a boil. Once the water was boiling hot, they dumped it into the pot where the frog was residing in. As a natural impulse reaction to the hot water being dumped into the pot, the frog quickly leaped out of the pot to avoid getting burned. In the second phase of the experiment, a frog was again placed into an empty pot. However, instead of dumping boiling water into the pot, the researchers had merely used room temperature water. The frog didn't react to the room temperature water as it had been used to liquids. However, the researchers placed the pot on top of a stove and gradually brought the water to a boil. Strangely, as the story goes, even as the water became hotter and hotter, the frog stayed in its place until it had succumbed to the heat and died.

Again, whether or not this was a real scientific experiment is irrelevant. The point here is that there are just some people who unknowingly place themselves in hot water and stay there for prolonged periods of time until it ends up killing them. This might be what happened to you. You might not have lost your job. You might not have lost a significant chunk of your savings to a bad business investment. You may not have had a pot of boiling water dumped on you. Perhaps, it was a series of choices that gradually led to the water around you getting hotter and hotter. The key now is for you to recognize the source of that heat so that you can make sure that you don't get boiled to death.

It's a simple matter of cause and effect. You know that currently, the effect is that you are struggling financially and that you need to make changes in your life. However, before you can make changes, you need to be able to pinpoint the causes of your financial struggles. This is not an easy feat as it's always going to differ from person to person. Not all people are going to make the same mistakes. However, there are indeed a few emerging patterns here that can make it easier for us to identify the common culprits. This chapter is going to take a deeper dive into the roots of the problem - your daily financial habits. You know that they say that your character is defined by your habits. That's true. In this sense, your financial character is defined by the kind of financial habits that you practice consistently. Sometimes, it's these bad habits that you do all too regularly that are digging your hole of struggle deeper and deeper.

Discipline and self-control are two very important traits for any fiscally responsible individual. However, you require a certain sense of self-awareness in order for you to really practice self control. The problem with a lot of people is that they don't even realize that they're doing things mistakenly before it's too late. This might be the case with you. It's possible that you understand that you're in hot water financially, but you might not necessarily be aware that you're still doing things that are keeping you in hot water. This is why self-awareness is vital when it comes to managing your money. You have to stay on top of whatever mistakes you might be committing with your finances so that you can do your best to avoid making them.

Ultimately, this chapter is going to be dedicated to developing your sense of self-awareness by making you more aware of how impactful your habits are on your financial situation. You might think that it's perfectly harmless for you to splurge on a luxury item once in a while. You might believe that it's okay for you to not invest in medical insurance. You might be under the impression that emergency funds are unnecessary. These are all fundamental financial mistakes that you're making and you need to be aware of that fact if you are to correct them.

After self-awareness comes humility. You need to be humble enough to acknowledge that you are doing things wrong and that you need to make that change. So, if you find that you are guilty of plenty of the things that are going to be listed in this chapter, own up to it. Be humble enough to admit that you have been making these mistakes and be responsible for your faults. Then, you can start to address these faults by changing your habits and correcting your behavior.

You Indulge in Overspending

The number one thing you have to avoid to make sure that you don't put yourself in debt is overspending. Simply put, you might be guilty of living outside of your means. Of course, there are many layers to overspending and there are a number of things that can contribute to you being guilty of it. For one, the world today is a very consumerist society. Everyone is pursuing material items and considering them to be essentials even when they're not. This has only been exacerbated by the prevalence of *flexing* on social media. Just because you see other people flaunting their expensive luxuries and belongings on social media may have influenced you to think that you are entitled to these things as well. So, you do whatever it takes to acquire these items even if it means you going broke in the process.

Companies and marketers don't make it easier for you to stop yourself from overspending either. Credit card companies are going to lure you in with all sorts of incentives like rewards, rebates, and low interest rates. Retail stores will try to spice up certain promos by offering discounted deals and *Buy One Get One* purchases. Again, it's a matter of psychology. When you aren't aware of the financial mistakes you're making, it can be very easy to get tricked into buying something that you don't need with money that you don't have. A lot of people have also come to rely on retail therapy for happiness. However, the stress that accompanies financial ruin always comes back around to bite them in the butt.

You Succumb to Peer Pressure

No. Just because a co-worker of yours bought a brand new car doesn't mean that you should do the same. Of course, it can be very tempting to do so. You know that you work in the same department and that you make relatively the same amount of money. In your mind, if they can afford a brand new car, then that means that you can afford it also. However, this is a wrong way to go about thinking about this kind of situation. First, you don't know if their job is their only source of income. Next, you never know what kind of other financial support he is getting for his car. Maybe he has parents who left him with a considerable trust fund to help him pay for such luxuries.

Also, you shouldn't feel pressured to keep up with your friends and their spending habits if you can't afford it. If your friends are planning to go on a vacation to some expensive destination that you know you can't afford, then just be upfront about it. Ask them if they would be willing to go somewhere more affordable. If not, then just don't tag along. There's no reason that you should be going broke just so you can feel included with the people you surround yourself with. After all, when you go broke, it's not like they're going to come and pay off your debts on your behalf. However, it doesn't even have to be with lavish luxuries like trips or vacations. Sometimes, even just consistently eating out at expensive restaurants can really add to your total expenses. It's okay to be a sociable person. Just make sure that you know your limits based on your finances.

You Don't Invest in Medical Insurance

Medical bills are no joke. At some point in your adulthood, you are going to have to accept the fact that you're not invincible and that you're prone to getting sick. It happens. This is not the kind of situation wherein you just cross the bridge when you get there. One of the biggest mistakes you could ever make is not investing in proper medical insurance. Many people seem to think that they don't have to worry about paying for medical expenses until they get sick. You shouldn't succumb to this kind of thinking. You just don't know how impactful a medical setback can be on your budgeting. Medical bills are huge burdens and they can really take a toll on a person's finances.

According to a 2017 study, the average cost per day at a hospital in the United States is $3,949 (Fay, 2017). That same report also said that average hospital stays cost an average of $15,734. Obviously, that is not a small number. Even if you have that kind of cash just lying around, you're still going to take a significant hit and it's going to hurt. More than 60% of all declared bankruptcies in the United States have something to do with medical bills.

Perhaps, the reason you didn't get medical insurance to begin with is because it was all too expensive for you. However, there are all sorts of medical insurance plans out there that are very much affordable and can have great pay-offs should you ever get sick. You shouldn't be intimidated. Regardless of the level of your income, there is an insurance plan out there that is right for you. It's merely a matter of you seeking out reputable insurance companies to make sure that you're investing your money in safe ventures.

You Don't Engage in Active Saving

You should always have a solid savings plan in place for yourself. The only way that you can really build up your savings is if you engage in active saving. One of the biggest mistakes that people can make is that they just do passive savings. They trick themselves into thinking that they are being financially responsible by setting aside a random amount of savings every week or month. However, this kind of absent-minded savings doesn't really work. It's always better when you are systematic with your method of saving. If you don't make an effort to save, then you're practically living paycheck to paycheck. That will become a serious problem whenever it's time for you to make certain unexpected transactions.

So, what does it mean to do passive saving versus active saving and why is the latter better than the former? When you do passive saving, you aren't practicing any discipline with regards to the money you set aside. You just take whatever available cash that you have and you put it into your savings account. Sometimes, if you don't have any extra available cash, then you don't have savings for that week or that month. Heck, you might even resort to dipping into your savings account every now and then to pay off certain expenses. This kind of passive saving is ineffective and will not serve you well in the long run.

Active saving is simple enough and can be explained rather clearly with an easy formula. With passive saving, the formula would be the following: *savings = income - expenses*. Essentially, you take your monthly income and you subtract all of your expenses from it. Whatever is left behind is going to be your savings. However, with active saving, it's a matter of flipping the equation. With passive saving, it's *income - savings = expenses*. So, with this kind of system, you take your monthly income and you immediately set aside a predetermined amount for your savings. Whatever money is left after that is what you have to play with for your expenses. It's up to you how much you should be setting aside every month. A general rule of thumb is that 20 percent of your monthly income should go to your savings. However, if you are capable of saving more than that, you should do so.

You Spend Money You Don't Have

We've already talked extensively about the idea of living on borrowed money. Just because you know that you have money coming in the future doesn't mean that it's okay for you to be buying things you can't afford right now. It would be incredibly foolish for you to put a down-payment on a house that you can't afford because you're anticipating that you will be promoted at your work within a couple of months. That would be a very irresponsible way of spending your money. Another example of this is buying an expensive luxury item like a nice dress in the middle of the month with your credit card. You don't have the cash for it, but you anticipate that you will have enough cash saved up by the time your credit card bill comes along. You can get away with this kind of spending only for so long.

Do not allow yourself to be lulled into a false sense of security just because you're anticipating an influx of cash coming your way. It would be much more prudent for you to act poor even when you know that your bank account says otherwise. One of the biggest mistakes that people make is that they prematurely act rich. What this means is that they know that they have the capacity to get rich in the future. So, they get ahead by trying to live the rich lifestyle even though they don't have the means to sustain it.

You Believe that Staying in Debt is Normal

To a certain extent, it's true. Debt is a very normal facet of society. However, a lot of people make the mistake of thinking that this means that it's okay to normalize debt in their own lives. It was already discussed in an earlier chapter about how not all debts are created equal. That still rings true. However, that's not an excuse for you to justify always having debt in your life. Just because you believe that you are accumulating good debt all the time doesn't mean that you're being smart with your money. There is absolutely no reason for you to normalize the presence of debt in your life. In fact, the key to achieving true financial independence in security is making sure that you have no outstanding debts or liabilities whatsoever.

Yes, there are some debts that can be useful. Sometimes, there are debts that are even necessary. However, you should be careful to not let it get to a point wherein you just become completely overloaded with debt. At the end of the day, good debt is still debt. You should be shooting for the kind of life wherein you aren't worrying about paying off any more debts or loans. To think that debt should play a permanent fixture in your life is one surefire way to put yourself on the road to eventual financial ruin.

You Don't Pay Your Bills On Time

This mistake can be summarized as a combination of overspending and buying into the belief that staying in debt is normal. There is nothing normal about you still having an outstanding balance at the end of every month. That's not how your finances should be looking like. When you have more liabilities than you do assets, that is often referred to as being in the red. This means that you owe more money than you actually have. Not paying your bills on time is a weird predicament to be in. Often, it's the result of you not being liquid enough to come up with the cash that you need to pay your bills. However, not paying your bills on time will also result in you incurring more penalties and fees that will have you paying more than you're supposed to. In that sense, it's almost like a double-edged sword.

One of the best ways to make sure that you constantly pay your bills on time is if you avoid committing a combination of mistakes that have been listed so far. If you are overspending, then you're going to have trouble paying your bills. If you don't engage in active saving, you will have trouble paying your bills. If you don't invest in medical insurance, you will have trouble paying your bills. See how there's a trend here?

Essentially, by committing a lot of the other mistakes that are listed here, you make it more difficult for yourself to pay your bills on time.

You Don't Make Smart Investments

We discussed earlier how overspending is bad and that you should avoid it if you want to be financially independent. Although, you shouldn't take that to mean that spending of any kind is bad. Just like debt, not all forms of spending are created equal. There is also such a thing as good investments and bad investments. Naturally, a common mistake that people make with their finances is when they engage in bad investments that yield minimal to no return. As much as possible, you should think of the money that you put out into the world as money that will eventually come back to you. If you have this kind of mindset when you're deliberating on what you're spending on, then it will be easier for you to maintain some sense of financial security.

All of the time, people are constantly making poor spending choices because they don't see their expenses as investments. For example, if you spend money on electricity, food, and running water, that's a good investment. After all, these are things that are crucial to your productivity and survival. Eventually, the money you pour into these things will return to you in the long run in the form of energy, good health, and productivity. If you invest in an expensive computer that you know will help you be more productive with your line of work, then that is a good investment. Eventually, if you use that computer to increase your income, then it was a purchase worth investing in. However, if you use that money to buy a computer just to play games and browse the internet with, then it might not necessarily be a good investment. You can buy a nice pair of leather shoes that you can use every day to wear to the office where you work. They might be expensive, but they're going to last you a long time. That's a good investment. Although, if you're using that money to buy an expensive pair of shoes just so you can look good at someone's wedding, then it isn't really a good investment because that money is never coming back to you.

Now, it's important to emphasize the point that you shouldn't necessarily be depriving yourself of occasional splurges and indulgences. It's okay to indulge in bad investments every once in a while if they're going to make you happy. However, if you know that you're strapped for cash and you really don't have that luxury at the moment, then you know it's a problem if you end up splurging. This is why the operative word of this piece of advice is making *smart* investments. You don't always have to be using your money for things that will yield high returns. There is always some room for a few bad purchases here and there. You just have to know your limits. Not all of your investments always have to be good ones. They just have to be smart ones.

You Go Through a Divorce

Divorces are really tough. Whenever you get married, you never really go into it thinking that you are going to eventually divorce the person you're with. Obviously, for the most part, when you get married, you have high hopes. You genuinely hope and believe that everything is going to work out for the best between yourself and your partner. Also, you make that commitment to one another and you really try to make things work. Although, the sad reality of the world is the fact that not all marriages last. It doesn't matter how much the two of you think you might love one another. The problems in a marriage can get very real and a lot of couples just end up calling it quits. While this is something that you would never want or anticipate for yourself, it's still important that you are prepared for it.

If you're lucky, you can have a clean and quick divorce that won't really cost you an arm and a leg. However, that's rarely ever the case. The legal fees that you rack up in a divorce can be crippling on your finances. This is especially true if your divorce proceedings aren't going smoothly and everything gets drawn out. Things get even more complicated if you are someone who is financially dependent on the person who is divorcing you. Now, you will be left to fend for yourself. You're going to be buried under a lot of legal fees to begin your new life after marriage too.

You Only Have One Revenue Stream

A really big and serious mistake that a vast majority of adults in the world make is believing that having just one revenue stream is enough. Most people go out and get jobs for themselves and they're content with that. They live off the salaries that they get from whatever company they decide to work for. However, this is a very unenlightened way to go about acquiring and handling money. Unbeknownst to many, there are actually three types of income: active, passive, and portfolio. *Active* income is the kind of income wherein you have to actively engage in some kind of labor in order for you to earn money. So, your level of active income is dependent on how much work you're putting in. *Passive* income is the kind of income that you get when you invest work at the start of a project and you have that investment pay off for you in the long-term. For example, if you invest in setting up an apartment building, the rent that you charge your tenants over an extended period will serve as your passive income. You're not necessarily actively working for this income, but you're still receiving it as the result of the initial work that you had put in at the start. Other examples of passive income include pensions, investment stakes, and royalties. Then, there is *portfolio* income. This is the kind of income that you can gain as a result of making good investments. Examples of portfolio income are the money that you get from dividends, capital gains, interest, and more.

It would be a big mistake if you limit yourself to just having active income. Sometimes, you will be put in certain scenarios wherein you will be unable to work. For instance, you might lose your job or you get sick. If you're just relying on active income, then you've practically lost all of your revenue streams. However, if you diversify your sources of income, then you always have other revenue streams to fall back on. Sometimes, this can mean you taking on another job for an extra source of active income. Other times, it may mean you investing in passive or portfolio forms of income.

You Don't Follow a Proper Budgeting System

The fact of the matter is that if you don't have a proper budgeting system, then you are never going to be able to balance out your finances. If you find yourself in a very deep financial hole, it's likely that you are there as the result of you having a poor budgeting system (or lack thereof). Also, there is no chance in the world that you would be able to pick yourself up from that whole without adhering to proper budgeting principles either.

You might be familiar with the whole adage about how failing to plan is also planning to fail. Well, your budget is essentially a plan for how you earn and spend your money. So, if you fail to plan the cash flow in your life, then you're also planning to fail in that regard. As uncomfortable or as tiring as it might be, it's important that you pay great attention to detail with handling your finances.

Most people seem to make the mistake of thinking that just because they're earning money, they can just practically buy whatever they want. There are limits to the money that you earn, so there should also be limits to the money that you spend. Having a solid budget plan in place is going to help you stick to those limits as much as possible.

You Just Lack a Grasp of Fundamental Financial Principles

Lastly, the biggest mistake that people could make with their money is just the choice to remain ignorant. We are currently living in the age of information. Any data or information that you might need about any topic in the world is readily available with just a few taps of your finger. You can gain access to a whole world of knowledge without even having to leave the chair that you're sitting in. There are so many people out there who remain financially ignorant and illiterate even though there's just no excuse for it anymore. On the internet, there is an absolute abundance of reading materials and collaterals that you could use to educate yourself on financial matters. It's merely a matter of you deciding to do so.

You can have all of the best intentions in the world with regards to your finances. However, if you don't have the necessary know-how to keep and grow your money, then all of your good intentions are moot. It's important that you take the time to really brush up on your financial literacy. Even if you just dedicated a couple of hours every week to studying your finances and learning more about how you can achieve true financial independence, it can go a long way. That's just not the case with most people. There are so many of us who just find financial management too boring, uninteresting, or not worthwhile. This is where the roots of the problems for a lot of people lie. Too many people still buy into myths and fake news about financial management. Not enough individuals are aware of the best practices and habits when it comes to investing and growing money.

Final Thoughts

If you find yourself guilty of a lot of these mistakes, you don't have to feel so bad. Yes, your mistakes in the past may have led you to a dark and scary place that you don't want to be in with regards to your finances. However, the bright light here is that you have managed to develop a sense of awareness of these mistakes. Again, the first step to solving a problem is recognizing that there is one. So, you're on the way to getting better. You're now starting to recognize what you're doing wrong so that you put yourself in a better position to do right.

Don't despair if you think that you're caught under the pressure of some very challenging circumstances. Sure, you've made your mistakes. However, these mistakes shouldn't get to define you. Just because you've committed these mistakes doesn't make you a failure. You're only a failure if you choose not to learn from the mistakes that you've committed in the past. You still have a shot at bettering your situation in spite of all your shortcomings. The purpose of writing this chapter wasn't to make you feel bad about everything that you've done. It wasn't about making you feel hopeless about how screwed up your situation might be. On the contrary, the purpose of this chapter was to make you realize that the problems you have right now are of your own doing. That means that you can change your situation by merely altering the way that you've been living up to this point. That should be your key takeaway from this.

Chapter 4: The Best Strategies to Get Out of Debt

We've come a long way thus far. By now, you should already have a clearer picture of the debt problem and how you got yourself in such a precarious position to begin with. However, the easy part is over. It's quite ironic, isn't it? It was probably so easy for you to fall into financial trouble. Heck, you might have not even been aware that you were doing so in the first place. It's a very effortless ordeal to fall into debt. It's not as if people design for themselves to be stuck under mountains of debts and loans. No one ever intends to be in that kind of situation. It's always something that happens by accident or by circumstance. So, yes, in that sense, it's very easy to fall into debt. It required very minimal effort on your part. Unfortunately, getting out of debt is a different story altogether.

You don't have to wait that long to be stuck in tens or even hundreds of thousands of dollars in debt. You would be able to achieve that feat in just a matter of months. Yet, when you're in the process of trying to balance your finances again, it can feel like an uphill battle that will wage on for years. Heck, there are some people who might even be paying off their debts in the spans of decades. Of course, that's neither here nor there. It doesn't matter how long it's going to take you to pay off your debts. The only thing that you have to remember here is to get started and to stay consistent. Otherwise, none of your efforts or desires are ever going to come to fruition.

You might already be getting to the point wherein you're just completely overwhelmed by the pressure that you're getting from your creditors. No one is going to blame you for feeling that way. It can really make for a tense environment whenever you know that you are indebted to other people. You don't get that sense of security that everyone craves for. It can be so anxiety-inducing when you're stuck in debt and you feel like you don't have a way out. However, there is always a way out for everyone. There is so much incentive for you to get out of debt. If you are just continuously allowing yourself to stay stuck in debt every single year, then you're only making it harder for yourself to climb back up. The sooner you act, the easier things will be for you. The sooner you get out of debt, then the more financial freedom you get in terms of diversifying and growing your wealth. When you are constantly bombarded with debt, it can feel very crippling. You are imprisoned by your own liabilities and you don't have the mobility to maximize the opportunities that would have been there for you if you weren't in debt. This is why it's important for you to plan for your next steps in terms of financial planning. This is precisely what this chapter is going to help you figure out.

You are more than capable of getting out of debt on your own. You just have to make sure that you're equipping yourself with the right tools to aid you in doing so. This chapter is going to provide you with a few general principles and tools that you should keep to heart to help you balance your finances. The path to financial independence isn't always going to be a straight line. It's not going to be a linear journey at all. For one, it's going to be different for everyone. Not all people are going to be going on the same paths and employing the same strategies to a tee. All situations are different and it's just a matter of scaling these principles and tips accordingly. Also, your success isn't going to be a smooth ride. You're going to experience a lot of ups and downs. It's almost like a weight loss journey. You might be successful at losing five pounds this week. Then, you just lose three pounds on the next. Suddenly, you find out that you gain one pound in the week after. It's going to be the same with your finances and that's okay. That's normal. There are going to be a few bumps on the road and you should be fine with that. Don't let it rattle you or shake your confidence. Again, the key here is to just get started and stay consistent.

You've already been able to identify the roots of the problem. That's the first phase. The previous chapters have already provided you with sufficient perspective on that front. Now, you just have to attack these problems head-on in a systematic manner. Don't worry if you're unsure of how you're going to go about that. This chapter will walk you through all of the best practices step by step.

Avoid Taking in More Debt

This should probably go without saying, but we're going to talk about it anyway. Try your best to avoid taking in more debt. When you know that you have a mountain to climb, the last thing that you would ever want to do is add more steps to that mountain. At the end of the day, it doesn't matter what kind of money-saving or budgeting tips you're going to employ. If you're in debt and you're continuously taking in more debt, you are just never going to get out of the hole. Again, this is a lot easier said than done. It's not like you ever wanted to find yourself in debt to begin with, right? This is exactly where discipline comes in. Sure, you're going to have to cut back and make some sacrifices here and there. You should be okay with that and come to terms with it.

You aren't going to be able to change your financial situation if you don't change your lifestyle. You have already been briefed on the many mistakes that you have been making which may have landed you in debt. You have also already been exposed to the many myths surrounding debt and finances. Use all of this newly learned knowledge to your advantage. Arm yourself with this information and make sure that you're not incurring any more debt than you already have. Starting today, calculate the total debt that you owe to your creditors. Once you have that number, make it a point that you never exceed that number again. Stop adding on to it. If it helps, you can even consider just cutting up your credit cards and throwing them away. You could also just call the banks and ask them to freeze your credit.

Pay More Than the Minimum

Again, it's a myth to think that you should only just be making minimum payments. You should try considering adding whatever money that you can set aside to clear your credit card balance. Even the littlest amount done on a consistent basis can go a really long way. As of this moment, no effort is too small. You might not think that merely adding $50 or $100 to your monthly payments can go a long way. However, you would be mistaken. It might seem like a rather simple solution, but over time, the results are definitely going to show. There's no need to exhaust this point even further here as it has already been debunked in the chapter of financial myths. However, to recap, the simple concept is that you end up saving yourself from paying higher interest fees when you're able to speed up the completion of your debt payments. In order for you to do so, you have to be willing to add in a little more money than is required every month.

Sure, in the short-term, it might feel like it's making a really huge dent in your spending power every month. This can be hard to go through when you know that money is tight and your spending is limited. However, in the long run, it's all going to work out for the better. You just have to be able to be patient and trust in the process. The gratification will come eventually.

Debt Consolidation

One of the biggest reasons that people feel like they are being overwhelmed with their bills and debts is that they are dealing with too many creditors. You might have all sorts of different loans that you are drowning in. It's possible that you are dealing with mortgages, car loans, student loans, and credit card debts all at once. Of course, it can be very hard to try to manage paying off all of these debts, especially when you only have one source of income. You end up having to funnel your money into many different pathways and you don't always know how to divide your cash intelligently. This is exactly where debt consolidation comes in.

To put it simply, debt consolidation is the act of taking all of the debts that you might have and gathering them all into a single payment. So, instead of funneling your cash to different pathways, you just have to merge all of your bills into one. This might seem like a difficult concept to grasp, but here's an oversimplified framework for how debt consolidation works. Let's say that you owe money to John, Jessica, and David. They all have varying interest rates and you owe them different amounts of money. Each creditor is giving you different terms to work with, and it's very confusing for you to figure out how to divide your finances properly to pay them off. Let's say that in total, you owe them $500. All you need is $500 and you would be able to pay all of them off and not have to deal with them ever again. To do this, you go to another creditor named Mary. You tell Mary that you want to borrow $500 from her and you'll pay her back on a monthly basis with interest. If Mary approves, you take the money she lends you and you immediately use it to pay off David, Jessica, and John. Now, you don't have to deal with those three creditors ever again. All you have to focus on is Mary. This will make it easier for you to manage your budget because you don't have to be dealing with so many variables.

Again, that's an oversimplification of the process, but it's just an illustration of how the idea of debt consolidation works. There are many ways in which you can choose to go about debt consolidation. However, these are the two most popular ways in which you can try consolidating your debt:

With a 0% Interest Credit Card

If you manage to find a credit card that offers 0% interest financing schemes, then you can make use of that to pay off all of your debts. Gather all of the existing debts that you have and charge them all to this credit card. Then, you just have to focus on making sure that you make timely and complete payments to your credit card within the promotional period so that you don't incur any additional interest.

With a Fixed-Rate Debt Consolidation Loan

If you don't have access to a 0% interest credit card promo, then you can always try to get a debt consolidation loan from a bank or any other creditor. With this method, you might have to prepare a few extra documents outlining the plans that you have with the loan. You might also have to prove that you are capable of paying your debt consolidation loan in full within a set amount of time. Typically, with this kind of loan, you just use the money they give you to pay off your debt to your other creditors. Then, you just have to focus on paying back this one loan over a set period through predetermined installment plans.

Other Forms of Debt Consolidation

There are also other ways in which you may try consolidating your debt such as home equity loans or 401(k) loans. Although, these kinds of loans do carry a certain amount of risk as they require your home or retirement fund as collateral. So, if possible, try to go for a loan with as minimal risk as possible. These are still very much valid forms of debt consolidation. There are also plenty of people who have managed to make it work. However, it all really depends on the situation. You just have to make sure that you take on the form of debt consolidation that works best for you.

Is Debt Consolidation Right for You or Not?

Debt consolidation is a very tricky and complex method of going about solving your debt problems. This is not necessarily a tip that is going to be available or applicable to everyone's situations. So, before you jump on the debt consolidation bandwagon, make sure that this is indeed the right path for you to take in alleviating your financial worries. As a general rule of thumb, here are some principles that you want to meet before you even start considering debt consolidation for yourself:

1. You have a credit standing that is good enough for you to gain access to 0% credit card or a low-interest debt consolidation plan. Otherwise, it might not be a good idea. If you have a high-interest debt consolidation agreement in front of you, you might end up having to pay a lot more money than if you just paid all of your debts individually.

2. You have a consistent stream of income that will help you make regular and timely payments. All of the hassles of getting a debt consolidation loan approved is going to be moot if you don't have the money to pay it off in the first place. Make sure that you are diversifying your revenue streams so that you always have money coming in which you can use to pay your debts.

3. You have a solid debt management plan in place to prevent you from taking on any more debt. It's foolish for you to try to consolidate all of your debts into one, and then you just go and take on other forms of debt for yourself. Again, you don't want to be adding to the mountain that you're already climbing.

If you need help figuring out whether a debt consolidation loan is right for you, there are various tools online that you can use to your advantage. The debt consolidation calculator found at https://www.bankrate.com/calculators/home-equity/debt-consolidation-calculator-tool.aspx can be a great tool to help you really crunch the numbers and determine what your best course of action should be.

Debt Settlement

Before anything else, it's important to emphasize that debt settlement is not the optimal solution for you to get out of debt. In fact, you should probably only ever consider this as a last resort and you feel like you have no other options available to you. You should only ever think about trying debt settlement if you know that you're in a desperate position and you really have no other means of paying your debts off. Consider this as your *Hail Mary* play before you settle on filing for bankruptcy. To put it simply, debt settlement is a method of you getting your creditors to accept a one-time, lump-sum payment to erase your debt. Sometimes, this can mean you won't pay the full amount and it's all dependent on whether creditors will agree to such terms. Usually, a creditor will only agree to a debt settlement if they see that you are on the brink of defaulting on your accounts.

There are two ways in which you might choose to go about debt settlement: by availing the services of a debt settlement company or on your own. If you choose to work with a debt settlement company, they will usually have you make incremental payments towards them as they build a sizable lump-sum that they can use to negotiate the terms of a settlement. Essentially, these companies serve as your representatives in making a case for your creditors to agree to a debt settlement. This is a convenience on your part as you are left to do minimal work. You merely have to give payments. However, this method can take time and you are also going to have to pay the fees set forth by these companies. Another option is that you just choose to build the lump-sum by yourself and negotiate the settlement on your own. Granted, it's a lot more work on your part but you have more control of the situation. Negotiations are hard and your creditors aren't always going to take it easy on you. This is why you shouldn't be pooling all of your efforts into a debt settlement as a primary solution.

Debt Snowballing

The debt snowball method is one of the most popular financial tools that people use to reduce their debts in a systematic manner. It provides a very structured framework and approach to tackling a variety of different debts and loans through a simple prioritization scheme. The way that debt snowballing works is that you just simply manage your finances and payments in such a way that your smallest and easiest debts get addressed first. The principle here is that you get rid of the smallest debt obligations first so that you gain the momentum and mobility that you need to take on the larger and more difficult debts. It's referred to as *snowballing* because you are starting small and are gradually adding snow to your ball as you make it bigger and bigger. In essence, you start small and you finish strong. It's the opposite of the *debt avalanche* method wherein you devise a financial system that addresses your biggest and largest debts first The problem with the debt avalanche system is that you don't get that burst of gratification that you need right away when you knock out a debt early. With debt snowballing, it's easier for you to immediately reap the fruits of your labor because you experience tangible success at a quicker rate.

With a debt snowball paying scheme, you are giving yourself a more structured approach to dealing with your finances. To perform debt snowballing properly, here are a few simple steps you need to follow:

Step 1: List Down All of Your Debts

The first thing that you need to do is write down all of your debts. Once you have all of your debts listed down, arrange them in order of size. Put the smallest debts on top and then arrange each of them accordingly with your largest debt on the bottom of the list. Then, beside each debt, assign the total monetary value for each one of them regardless of interest rates.

Step 2: Plot Your Payment Scheme

Once you have all of your debts in plain view, it's now time to start budgeting your payments accordingly. Except for the very first item on your list, budget your money in a way that you are making minimum payments for every single debt. Just stick to the bare minimum. Then, for the first item on your list, assign as high a dollar value as you possibly can. Commit to the highest possible amount that you would be able to pay that particular creditor on a consistent basis. Execute this payment scheme every single month until the initial debt is paid off.

Step 3: Repeat the Snowballing Method Until All Your Debts are Gone

Once the first debt is paid off in full, repeat the second step of the snowballing method with the next item on the list. Continue this process over and over again until all of your debts have been repaid.

Debt Calculator

Again, if you're having trouble crunching the numbers, there are various tools online that can help you out. The calculator at https://www.nerdwallet.com/blog/finance/what-is-a-debt-snowball/ can help you determine if the snowballing method could possibly work effectively for your financial situation. Just make sure that whatever plan you decide on is a plan that you can stick to. It's much better to stay consistent on a plan that has minimal payoff than to abandon a plan that's just too complicated to work with.

The Art of Renegotiation

Sometimes, it really pays to just ask. Keep in mind that previously, we discussed how it's a myth that your banks or creditors don't care about whether you are able to make payments or not. That is far from being true. In fact, they would much rather have you be able to pay your debts off than have your debts be defaulted. So, you can make the argument that they are deeply invested in you being able to succeed in paying your debts off in full. This is why it would be a good idea for you to try to reach out to your bank and ask if it's okay for you to renegotiate the terms of your debt. The truth is that it's not a rare occurrence for people to be phoning in their banks and asking for easier payment terms. If you genuinely feel like your interest rates are too high, you can call your bank and ask them to renegotiate the terms of your debt. If you are able to prove that you have a good reputation for making payments on time, then you are going to have higher chances of them taking it easier on you. They would much prefer to do this than to have a debt settlement.

Moreover, this isn't just a tactic that you can use for your credit card debts. There are different kinds of bills and payments that you can try to renegotiate as well. Again, at the end of the day, you have nothing to lose when you try to negotiate with your creditors. The worst possible scenario is that they say no and you're just back to where you are now. Some examples of regular payments that you can try to renegotiate are monthly rent, medical bills, internet service, and the like. A lot of people are so familiar with the idea of trying to negotiate a salary raise with their bosses. This is good. You should always look to up your level of income. However, there's nothing wrong with you employing the same tactic when you're trying to lower your expenses as well.

Balance Transfers

Unfortunately, it's not all the time wherein your negotiation skills are going to come through to you. You tried, but you failed. You asked your credit card company to go easier on you with the interest rates, but they were stern. They didn't like what you had to say and so you're back to square one. If that's the situation that you have found yourself in, you can now resort to the option of a balance transfer. This kind of works within the same realm of debt consolidation, except you're just really using another credit card to pay off your current credit card debts. Again, it's not very wise for you to incur any more debt when you're trying to get out of debt. So, it would seem counterproductive to pay off a current debt by taking on another kind of debt, right? That's true. However, there is a way to make this work. You just have to make sure that you execute everything properly.

You just have to try to find another credit card that offers a balance transfer option with 0% interest. Some companies offer 0% APR for as long as 12 or 18 months. Most of these companies will enforce some kind of balance transfer fee in order for you to avail of such a service. However, if all of the math works out, it might end up being the better option for you. Again, just make sure that you do all of your due diligence and that you really study up beforehand. Read the fine print and familiarize yourself with every single detail of the deal. If in doubt, try consulting a financial advisor or expert on the specifics of the deal. If everything works out for you, then it's going to be a much easier burden to carry moving forward.

Practice Responsible Credit Card Usage

If you're struggling to get out of debt, one of the best things that you could possibly do is to just stop using your credit card. Again, you should always think of the credit card as money that you don't have yet. More importantly, it's money that you might not ever have. So, any purchase that you make on your credit card isn't done with money that's yours. It's borrowed money and we've already talked about how bad that could be for you. So, for now, if you feel like you really can't control yourself with your credit card usage, then just set it aside and stop using it.

However, there will be times wherein credit card deals or rebates might be too good to pass up. They might be so good that it would really make better fiscal sense to use your credit card instead of cash. If that's the case, then this is what you need to do. Every single time you use your credit card on a purchase, withdraw the same amount of money from your debit account and set that cash aside. Consider that as money lost and don't touch that money until the end of the month when it's time to pay your bills. This way, you're using your credit card, but you're also making sure that you're using your own cash that you have on-hand. This is the best kind of credit card usage that ensures that you're not living on borrowed money.

Diversify Your Revenue Streams

Regardless of who you are or what kind of job you have, it's very important that you diversify your revenue streams. Gone are the days wherein people can just rely on working at their nine-to-fives to sustain them all throughout life. The only real and practical way you can achieve financial independence as a self-made person is if you diversify your revenue streams or win the lottery. However, how many people do you know have won the lottery? You shouldn't have to rely on luck to make your fortune. You need to put in the work and the dedication needed to increase the level of your income. A lot of the time, working a single job is not going to be enough to do that.

Sure, in order for you to get out of debt, the most important thing that you need to do is to limit your expenses. When you're not spending your money, then you have that money on-hand to use as a security blanket. It's also a lot easier to pay off your debts when you're not spending your cash on other things. However, it shouldn't just be about you limiting your expenses. It should also be about you trying to bring more money home at the end of the day. There are so many different things that you can do to diversify your revenue streams depending on your level of risk. Earlier, it was discussed that there are many different forms of income such as active, passive, and portfolio. You should try to see if you would be able to maximize these different types of income to raise the amount of money that you're bringing home with you.

Make Use of Budgeting or Money-Saving Tools

With the advent of technology, there are myriad different tools and platforms that you can use to help you manage your budget or finances better. These days, the tech industry has probably come up with some kind of a solution to practically any kind of world problem. Naturally, with the sheer amount of people who are experiencing financial troubles these days, the tech experts have deemed it necessary to come up with a few budget management and money-saving tools that could prove to be useful for the layman. In fact, there are so many different apps and platforms out there that are designed to serve this purpose. Don't worry. You won't have to browse through all of them. Here is a carefully curated list of a select few that you might want to keep your eyes on to help you with your budgeting. After all, you need all the help you can get. If that help comes in the form of an app, then you should be willing to take it.

YNAB or EveryDollar

YNAB or *You Need a Budget* is an all-around budgeting app that is easy to use and offers a variety of features. With the way that the app is designed, every user is encouraged to create a monthly budget. All of this can be done within just a few minutes too. On top of that, the app is also programmed to have you live off the earnings of a previous month instead of money that has yet to come your way. This way, you're not living off money you don't have yet. Unfortunately, YNAB is a paid app and it might not be good if you're really trying to cut down on expenses.

EveryDollar is the perfect free alternative to YNAB. EveryDollar carries most of the same features, but it doesn't have as clean or intuitive an interface. Also, there is a paid version of EveryDollar that gives you more customizability in your app usage.

Personal Capital

For those who are really looking to get into the more advanced and intermediate aspects of money management, Personal Capital can help you out. It's a free-to-use app that primarily functions as an investment tool. This is good for those who are really looking to diversify their revenue streams and who want to grow their money. However, aside from that, it also has a few money management features like transaction tracking, debt monitoring, and more.

Mint

If you want a budgeting tool that is free, simple, straight to the point, and easy to use, then Mint is the one for you. It is programmed to automatically update and categorize any transactions that you make. So, you get instantaneous updates and reports on your spending habits as they happen in real time. In addition to that, Mint is also capable of providing you with free credit score assessment and monitoring services. It's a great no-fuss app that is loaded with features and is free to use.

Clarity Money

Clarity Money is another budgeting app that has all of the basic features like expense tracking and savings monitoring. It's also able to seamlessly link into all sorts of accounts from financial institutions so that you are able to get real-time updates on the states of your finances. More than that, Clarity Money also offers credit score monitoring and subscription canceling features as well.

Google Spreadsheet/Microsoft Excel

If you're the type who wants to take a barebones approach to managing your finances, then a simple spreadsheet will do just fine for you. In this spreadsheet, you could choose to input all of the details surrounding your financial situation. Make sure that you are tracking everything. Take note of every single dollar that you spend and earn. Also, this is a good way for you to always stay on tops of what debts you owe, what bills you have to pay, and what money you have coming in.

Get Rid of Non-Essential Subscriptions

Spotify. Netflix. Sports Illustrated magazines. Gym memberships. These are all examples of common subscriptions that people have in their daily lives. Sure, maybe a single Spotify subscription might not make that big of a dent on your finances. Although, if you add all of these things up, it can really make an impact on the way that you're spending your money. Be honest with yourself with regards to whether you really need these subscriptions or not. At the end of the day, when you're in trouble financially, you only want to be spending on the necessities. Given that, would you consider Spotify to be a necessity? Do you really NEED that gym membership? These are all questions that you need to ask yourself to make sure that you are only spending your money on the absolute essentials. Otherwise, it might be best to cut ties with these subscriptions that are eating away at your monthly budget.

Cut Down on the Luxuries

Lastly, you just need to make sure that you cut down on whatever luxuries you might have in life. When you're in financial trouble, it is not a good time to be luxurious. This might be particularly difficult for those who may have grown accustomed to a certain lifestyle. Understandably, making very dramatic lifestyle changes aren't going to be easy. However, if you really want to improve your current situation, you need to be honest with yourself in the evaluation of your spending habits. Really make an effort to be anal about it too. Don't just look at the big picture stuff. Really try to focus on all the littlest details. Wherever you are able to cut back on spending, do so. You might not think much of that cup of coffee that you get from Starbucks three to five times a week. However, if you add all of that up over the course of the year, that money could have gone to significantly cutting off a huge chunk of your debt.

As difficult as this might be to hear, luxuries are only reserved for the financially stable. Obviously, if you're reading this book, then you are not that person. As blunt as it might sound, this is exactly the kind of reality check that you need. Try to cut back as much as possible on the indulgences that you have. Only when you consider yourself out of the woods and in the clear can you start to think about treating yourself again. Remember that one probable reason you're in the hole that you are in now is because you have been overindulgent. In order for you to get out of that hole, discipline must take over.

Chapter 5: The Simple Secrets to Staying Out of Debt

Earlier, we drew a minor comparison between getting out of debt and losing weight. There are actually a lot of parallels to be drawn between these two endeavors. Like it is with getting into debt, no one ever intends on getting fat. No one becomes overweight by accident. It's always going to be the result of minor bad nutrition and lifestyle choices that are done consistently. These consistent poor choices accumulate and eventually lead to a person becoming obese. Getting into debt (for the most part, save for unforeseen emergencies) is a lot like that as well. You don't get into debt by splurging on just a single luxury handbag or one expensive meal. It's usually a succession of poor financial choices that can lead to you getting into deep debt.

Also, we talked about how getting out of debt is a lot like losing weight in the sense that success is never linear. You are going to experience a few setbacks every now and then. You will have your shortcomings along the way. In spite of your best efforts, the plans that you draw up to better your life might not always work out the way that you envision them to. This is why it's important to adapt. Show a willingness to change things up and try alternative methods of improving your situation. If debt consolidation isn't right for you, then maybe you can try debt snowballing. When you're trying to lose weight, if a low-carb diet isn't working for you, then maybe you can try intermittent fasting instead. There is no one true solution to getting out of debt the same way that there is no one solution to losing weight. It's always going to be different for everyone.

Now, you might be asking yourself, why is there so much talk about losing weight when we're just talking about money and budgeting here? Well, that's because there are certain principles and lessons that you can draw from one which you can also apply to another. One such example is withdrawal or falling off the wagon. You've probably seen it happen to a lot of people who have lost a significant amount of weight. These are people who got really fat and then they decided to turn their lives around. With enough grit, determination, conviction, and hard work. They are able to do so. They are able to accomplish their goals and reach their desired metrics with regard to their weight. Some of these people are able to maintain their healthy lifestyles and they keep their weight off. However, there are also a lot of people who get complacent as a result of their success. They lose focus and they cease to keep their eyes on the ball. When that happens, they gradually slip into a decline and before they know it, they find themselves back where they started. They're overweight again and they have to repeat the entire process of losing weight once more.

Now, this is something that you might not think applies to people who manage to get out of debt. Although, as they say, old habits die hard. You never want to find yourself back in the hole that you tried so desperately to escape from. This is precisely the kind of situation that this chapter is going to try to help you avoid as well. In the previous chapters, you were exposed to the many factors and bad habits that contributed to your financial demise. Fortunately, you were also given various tools and tips on how you could better your situation in spite of the odds that were stacked against you. If you're lucky, then you've already achieved some sense of financial health and stability with the help of everything that you've learned so far. Currently, the job is now for you to make sure that you keep things that way. You've lost all of the excess fat. It's now time for you to maintain that weight or to get even leaner, if possible.

Embrace Frugality

Think rich, but act poor. Internalize the principle of frugality. In life, you should shoot to be as productive as possible. Whenever you can, try to monetize that productivity so that you always have healthy streams of money flowing into your bank account. Along the way, you will want to supplement your productivity with various essentials like food, clothing, shelter, and whatnot. When doing so, make sure that you practice frugality as much as possible. Why pay $35 for a gourmet cheeseburger when you can make the same thing at home for less than $10? Why would you spend $300 on a pair of sneakers when you can get another pair that's just as nice and sturdy for $50? Essentially, wherever you have an opportunity to minimize your expenses, then make the most out of it.

Here are a few examples of certain things in your life that you don't want to be overindulging in:

- restaurant meals
- cell phone plans
- clothes and accessories
- subscription plans
- credit card membership fees
- movies, concerts, and other such events
- daily coffee
- private car/cab rides
- drinks, etc.

Now, it's important to note that you don't have to eliminate these things entirely. Of course, no one can be productive without a proper cell phone plan these days, right? No one is asking you to give up any of these things. It's just a matter of cutting costs whenever you can. So, instead of paying for a premium phone plan that allows you to have unlimited minutes and premium data privileges, try downgrading to a simpler and more minimalist plan. If you take this kind of approach to everything you're spending money on, you're going to end up saving a lot of cash.

Be Strict with Budgeting

As cliché as it sounds, think of running your household as you managing a business. When you manage your business, you want to make sure that you stay as profitable as possible. How do you do this? It's a simple matter of making sure that there is more money coming in than there is going out. In order for you to sustain a business, you need to deal with certain expenses. This means that money has to go out of your business to be invested in things like salaries, real estate, technology, research, and whatnot. All of those things are vital to the survival and success of a business, so they are worthwhile investments. However, what makes these things worthwhile are sales. Businesses need to meet specific sales numbers in order to keep money coming in. Now, the most successful businesses are most concerned with widening the gap. What gap is being talked about here? The gap is the numerical distance between the money that is going out and money that is going into a business. As much as possible, you want to minimize your expenses while maximizing your sales. The best and most successful businesses in the world are masters at widening that gap.

This is the kind of approach that you need to take when you're budgeting for your household as well. Yes, there are certain expenses in your household that you consider essentials. You need to pay for electricity, groceries, internet service, furniture, and whatnot. Think of these as necessary investments to keep your household running smoothly. After all, this is your place of rest and sanctuary. Every man or woman needs a home. This is where you can recharge and re-energize yourself so that you are prepared to go to work and earn a living. Some people even don't have to leave their homes to bring home the bacon. Think of everything that you do in your career as the sales of your business. When you do good at work, that means you're bringing in more money into your *business*. You're generating more sales that you can invest right back into your home and your lifestyle. Given that, it's important that you are able to widen the gap between your expenses and your earnings as much as possible. The only way that you are able to do that is if you stay strict with your budgeting.

In the previous chapter, you were educated on various apps and tools that you can use to your advantage to make sure that you are engaging in proper budgeting. When you have proper budget management tools and systems in place, then you minimize the chances of you spending more than you're earning. Be strict with yourself and widen that gap.

Stick to a Shopping List

Be honest with yourself. How many times have you ever gone to the mall with the intention of picking up just one or a few items only to return home with a lot of extra fluff? It's so easy when you're heading out to just get sidetracked with a lot of side missions. This is a big no-no when you're supposed to be living a frugal and financially minimalist lifestyle. Whenever you head out with the intention of buying something, make sure that you stick to your plans. So, let's say you're out because you need to go shopping for office clothes, then just stick to that. Prepare a list of specific items that you need and stick to that list as much as possible. For example, say that you only need to buy two pairs of slacks and three different kinds of shirts because that's all you have budgeted for. Don't get distracted by buying jackets, socks, shoes, and whatnot on the side. These are extra expenses that don't fit within your plan and are not a part of your budget.

Do the same with groceries as well. When you go to the grocery store, make sure that your list is ready even before you leave the house. Once you reach the store, only add items that are already on your list. If you find something that catches your eye and isn't on your list, ignore it. Instead of buying it now, incorporate that item into the budget for your next round of groceries in the next month. This way, you are always sticking to your budget every single time you leave the house to spend your money.

Be Open to Talking About Your Finances

One of the most prominent reasons that so many people remain illiterate or ignorant when it comes to financial responsibility is that not enough people are open to talking about money. Even in a simple family setting, it's very taboo for a lot of people to talk about money in the house. That's a real problem because it doesn't address the issue of finance in a realistic and pragmatic manner. When you're one of the people who is making money in the household, it's very important that you discuss your finances with your partner. Even if you're the only one who is making money for your family, it's still important that you and your partner have open conversations about the state of your finances. If you are a parent, you also have to take it upon yourself to educate your kids about money as well. This way, they also have the tools that they need to arm themselves against falling into financial ruin.

Also, talking about finances with the members in your family is good for setting expectations. You always want your family to be aware of the struggles you might be going through in acquiring and keeping your money. This way, they will also do their parts in making sure that they are responsible with the handling of the household's finances.

Be Honest With Yourself

You must always be honest with yourself. Don't try to trick yourself into thinking that your bad spending habits are okay. Stop forcing yourself to believe that you are worthy of luxury items even though you can't afford them. Honesty and realism is very important when it comes to maintaining financial security and independence. When you have an overly optimistic view of how much money you have and your capacity to bring more money in, then that could spell trouble for you in the future. You might really end up tricking yourself into believing that you can afford to buy things that you can't.

At the start of this book, it was mentioned that a lot of financial management and responsibility has to do with psychology. It's not just about the pluses and minuses. Sure, mathematics come into play here when you're trying to balance your checkbook. However, for the most part, it's really about your mental fortitude. Your honesty and discipline will help you make better decisions and forge stronger financial habits that will help keep you out of debt. If you really struggle with developing your mental strength in handling your money, then it might be wise for you to seek the professional advice of a financial advisor or even a psychologist. Either way, there's no shame in trying to seek professional help from someone who is in a position to make you a better person overall.

Don't Buy Anything You Can't Pay Off in 30 Days

Don't buy anything that you can't afford. It doesn't matter how sweet a deal might be. You shouldn't care about how much you're saving by buying a particular item at that moment. If you can't afford it, then you shouldn't even be thinking about buying it. If it's a rather large purchase, then maybe you might need to take some time to sit with it for a bit. Sure, you might be able to afford that huge LED TV that would look great in your living room. However, this is not the kind of purchase that you want to be making on a whim. You have to go back home and sleep on it. Do your research on that particular TV and see if you can scout for better deals elsewhere. After a few days of thinking about it and weighing out all the pros and cons, if you feel like it's a wise purchase, then go for it. This is what you call mindful purchasing.

A lot of the time, when something catches your eye when you're online shopping or when you're at the mall, it can be very tempting to just pull the trigger. However, you have to keep in mind that these products are well-marketed and are designed for you to be tempted to make an impulsive decision even though it might be against your best interest. So, just to make sure that you aren't caught up in the hype of marketing, just say no immediately and take some time to think about it first. As a general rule, you want to avoid making impulsive purchases on anything that you have to finance or can't pay off in the span of 30 days. If you can't afford to pay for something in 30 days, then just walk away and think about it for a bit. Better yet, come back when you have saved up enough and see if you still want it at that point.

Find Someone to Keep You Accountable

There's an old African proverb that goes, "If you want to go fast, go alone. If you want to go far, go together." And this is an adage that applies to finance as well. Sure, when you're trying to sort things out with your finances, it can be a lot more efficient if you're just doing it on your own and you don't have anyone distracting you. You don't have to listen to the thoughts, advice, and opinions of others. This means that you're free to just do whatever you want and get the job done in no amount of time. However, by doing this approach, you are also depriving yourself of valuable perspective and insight from people who might know more than you. By isolating yourself, you are putting yourself at a disadvantage.

Whenever you can, try to find someone who can help keep you accountable to your financial responsibilities and duties. Sometimes, this person can take the form of a romantic partner, a colleague, or even a financial advisor. Whatever the case, it's always good when you have someone there who serves as your watchman. This way, there is a certain level of external pressure that will help you stay disciplined. Also, it's more sustainable when you know that you're going through financial difficulties with someone. The empathy and support that you get from another person will go a long way in helping you achieve your financial goals.

Make Prompt and Timely Payments

At this point, you should probably already know just how important it is to make your payments within schedule. When you're constantly being bombarded with late payment fees, it can be very easy for you to end up falling back into debt. You never want that to be the case. These late payment fees are unnecessary expenses and they're a waste of valuable resources. If you want, make use of an app that will help remind you whenever you are nearing the deadline of a bill payment. One might not think much of it, but paying bills on time can go a really long way in helping you stay out of debt.

There are certain companies that allow for automated bill payments straight from your bank account. This way, you won't even have to worry about making payments at all. You just have to make sure that your account is always filled with the appropriate amount of cash.

Build Your Emergency Fund

At the base of it all, there is only one thing in the world that will be able to keep you out of debt: money. When you have enough money, then you have a shield that will help make sure that you never end up owing anyone anything. So, how do you build up that kind of formidable defense against debt? You need to have a respectable savings fund.

Regardless if you're in the process of trying to get out of debt or if you've just freshly gotten out of it, it's important that you continuously build on your savings fund. A savings fund is a war chest. It's something that you just whip out anytime you are faced with an emergency situation. Also, if you've just gotten out of debt, it's a lot easier for you to focus on building your savings. All of the money that would have gone to paying off student loans or credit card bills can now go into your savings.

If you don't have a savings fund yet, then make one. Remember that the best time to start saving is always yesterday. So, if you're not saving today, then you're already behind. When you're just starting out, shoot for more tangible and feasible goals. Depending on your income, you want to set up milestones for yourself so that you always have something to shoot for. A modest first milestone would be to develop a war chest with around $1,000 in it. This is a good place to start with regards to your emergency fund. It's not that big of an amount that would have you chasing after it for too long. However, it's also not small enough of an amount that it wouldn't really be able to make a difference should an emergency arise. Even when you're not earning that much, so as long as you stay disciplined and aren't paying off any debts, you can reach $1,000 in no time.

Then, you can gradually start to evolve your goals and build your war chest. Upgrade your milestone to $2,000. Then, make it $3,000. If you're feeling ambitious, bump it up to $5,000. Just think of your war chest as your own personal safety net. The bigger your emergency savings, then the less likely you are ever going to fall back into debt. Now, having $5,000 in your emergency fund is good for making sure that you're covered for small emergencies like car repairs or minor home renovations. However, this might not be a big enough amount to cover major emergencies like unexpected unemployment or medical issues. Depending on who you ask, the ideal amount for an emergency fund will vary. However, the general consensus seems to be that your emergency fund should be enough to pay for around three to six months' worth of expenses. If you are a truly financially responsible individual, then you would be very much aware of how much money you're spending on a monthly basis. Now, multiply that amount by three to six, and that should be what you're aiming for with regards to your emergency fund. So, if you ever find yourself without a job all of a sudden, you have around three to six months to pick yourself back up on your feet again without having to worry about going into debt. If you're lucky enough to be able to build an emergency fund that surpasses that amount, then go ahead. Again, the key here is to minimize expenses and maximize savings as much as possible.

Chapter 6: Starting Your Savings - The Real Secret of Making Money Work for You

There are certain layers to financial stability. Ground zero is you not having any debt, but also not having any savings to work with. The next level after that is you having a solid budgeting system with a respectable savings account to make sure that you're safe from any unexpected emergencies or pitfalls. Now, once you've reached that level, you shouldn't stay content. Remember the whole principle of widening the gap between your expenses and your income? This is what you need to constantly focus on once you're out of debt.

One very effective way of widening that gap is investing your money properly. You have to know that you can put your money into positions wherein they start working for you. Instead of you working hard every day to earn your cash, you can choose to invest your cash and have them multiply on their own. If you're very strategic about it, you can start to grow your wealth to heights that you would never have dreamed of when you were struggling with your debt. It doesn't even matter if you don't have that much money to invest in the first place. Everyone has to start somewhere. It's just a matter of making the right investment choices every day so that your money continues to grow.

Again, there are very few things in life that will feel as good as you knowing that you don't have to think about where you need to source some cash to pay off your expenses. You can go to sleep at night knowing that you will have enough cash to pay for your kids' tuition, groceries, utilities, and even some occasional luxuries. That's the goal that you should be shooting for with regards to your finances. The best way for you to get to that level is to take whatever disposable income that you have and invest it in some worthwhile opportunities.

If you know squat about investing, then don't worry. Not too many people do. This is part of why so many people struggle with keeping themselves afloat financially. This chapter is going to educate you on some very basic principles and concepts behind investing. In this manner, you are always putting yourself in the best possible position to achieve whatever financial goals you might set for yourself and those you love.

Build Your Investment Fund

The very first step to investing your money is building an investment fund. Now, it's very important to emphasize that your investment fund is different from your emergency funds. You always need your emergency funds to be readily available for when... well, emergencies arise. Whatever money that you choose to put into an investment fund should be considered as money lost. So, make sure that you budget accordingly. Treat your investments as you would an expense.

The answers are going to differ depending on who you ask. However, a good rule of thumb to follow with regards to budgeting for investments is to just take 10% of your income. So, if you earn $5,000 a month, then just set aside $50 to add to your investment fund. If you feel like you want to be more aggressive in your investing, then you can increase that amount. It's up to you. What's important is that you decide on an investment budget that you're comfortable with. Again, this is money that is designed to grow, but you shouldn't expect to get it back after a long while.

If you want, you can make use of an app like Revolut which automatically sets aside a portion of your monthly income into a digital vault. Think of this as forced savings for your investment fund.

Research on Different Investment Options

Once you are able to build up a sizable and respectable investment fund, it's now time for you to put your money where your mouth is. Now, this book isn't going to go into specific details on how you should be investing your money. Rather, you will be presented with a list of investment options, and you are free to choose how you want to invest your cash. Although, one piece of advice that you should take to heart is that you should try to diversify your portfolio. This is all in accordance with the principle of not putting all of your eggs in one basket. No matter how much research you put into investing, there is always a chance that an investment can fail. So, if you pour all of your funds into a single investment and it fails, then you're left with nothing to play with. However, if you place modest amounts of money into different investment opportunities, then you're making it safer for yourself to earn money in the long run.

Savings Account

There's a reason why people shouldn't be keeping their money under their beds and that reason is called inflation. If you have one hundred dollars and you choose to just keep it under your bed, you will end up losing money more and more each day. How does that work? Through inflation. The hundred dollars you have today isn't going to have the same kind of spending power in one, two, five, or ten years' time. Because of inflation, commodities are always going to rise in terms of expense. This is why the spending power of your one hundred dollars is going to diminish over time.

So, instead of keeping your money under your bed or in a piggy bank, store it in a savings account. Try to research on the banks that offer the highest compounding interest. Compounding interest is essentially the returns on investment that you get when you pour your money into a savings account. However, keep in mind that these returns are very minimal and might not even be up to par with inflation rates.

Certificates of Deposit

A Certificate of Deposit is an agreement that you make between yourself and a bank. With this kind of agreement, you give the bank a certain amount of money for a fixed amount of time. Then, based on the terms of the agreement, the bank will return that money to you once the agreement has concluded along with your interest earnings. With this kind of investment scheme, the longer you lend your money to the bank, the more money you get in return. This is a very safe and risk-free way of investing your money. You won't ever have to worry about losing money with this method of investment.

However, there are some caveats to this kind of investment as well. For one, you don't get to withdraw your money back throughout the duration of the agreement. This means that you can't have access to this money should an emergency arise. Also, you might miss out on other more valuable investment opportunities if all of your funds are locked up with the bank. Lastly, the returns on a CoD are very minimal as well and might not be able to keep up with the rates of inflation.

Stocks

Have you ever dreamed of owning companies like Apple, Nike, or Disney? Well, you can! You can claim to own shares of these companies and more through the stock market. So, the way that stocks work is that you invest your money into these companies. In return, they will give you shares. These shares entitle you to partial ownership of the companies. Sometimes, this entails you receiving occasional dividends as well. Dividends are sums of money that are paid out to the shareholders of a company on a regular basis with the use of profit or reserves. However, this is not the only way you can earn money with stocks.

When you invest your money into shares for a certain company, they will take that money and invest it into measures to grow their business. The higher the growth for a business, then the more valuable that money becomes. Hence, they end up getting higher stock prices. So, let's say that you bought a single share of Microsoft for one dollar. If Microsoft plays its cards right and continues to experience economic growth, then its stock values will become higher as the years go by. If you check back on the stock market after five years, it's possible that a single share of Microsoft stock will now cost $15 dollars because of their growth as a company. So, your investment of $1 has now grown in value to $15. You can now opt to sell your share and earn your profit or leave your money there and allow it to grow even further.

The pros with the stock market is that it's a relatively safe investment if you do proper research and if you're investing in good companies called *blue chips*. Blue chip stocks are typically companies that have a proven track record for growth and have minimal risk. However, the cons of investing in the stock market is that it can take quite some time before you see significant returns on your investment.

Bonds

To put it simply, investing in a *bond* means that you're turning yourself into a lender. There are various entities and institutions out there that will offer you a bond for a fixed amount. If you agree to this bond, then you hand over your money to them. Then, in order to grow your money, they lend this out to people who are looking for loans. Through the interest rates that are placed on these loans, you would be able to yield profitable returns on your investment depending on the terms of your bond.

Bonds are practically risk-free and that's their biggest selling point. Let's say that you establish a bond deal with a company that has you being paid 5% interest over the span of 10 years. After 10 years, when you collect, you are entitled to that 5% regardless if the bond company has performed well over the years or not. However, you are also locked into that period and you have no access to that money for that set duration. Also, if a bond company experiences a dramatic growth, you are not entitled to anything beyond the terms of your investment. Even if they grow 25% in 10 years, you are still only entitled to the 5% that you agreed upon.

Mutual Funds

Consider a mutual fund as a pool of investments that come from yourself and from other people. The company that is handling the mutual fund will take your money and the money of others and invest it into many different opportunities. Essentially, with mutual funds, you are taking your money and investing it in many different outlets. This way, you are diversifying your portfolio and minimizing your risk. If one of those investments doesn't turn out well, at least you have the other investments to help you come out on top.

Aside from that, mutual funds are more accessible in the sense that you can get your money back faster as compared to bonds or CoD. However, the longer you leave your money in those funds, then the higher your returns will be.

Consider Micro-investing

If you don't want to put up a huge amount of cash to pour into major investments, then you can always resort to micro-investing instead. As its name implies, micro-investing is the act of contributing small amounts of money into an investment opportunity or brokerage account. Depending on the nature of the micro-investment platform, the money can be invested in a number of different ways.

Uniquely, micro-investing apps nowadays are programmed to take whatever digital *loose change* you might have and use them for investments. For example, you can link your bank account or e-wallet to your micro-investing platform. You go out and you buy a cup of coffee, and you use your phone to make the transaction. In this case, let's say the cup of coffee costs $2.50 and you paid $3 for it. You can program your micro-investing app in a way that the remaining $0.50 goes into your micro-investing fund. Now, this is just a very minor example. However, if you do this consistently enough, you will have amassed a sizable investment fund for yourself just by going about your usual daily transactions.

Of course, the pros of this kind of investment is that it's very intuitive and hassle-free. No one ever likes carrying around loose change anyway. At least you're putting all of this loose change into a real and tangible investment. However, the con remains that these are micro-investments and they yield micro-returns as well. Better something than nothing?

Conclusion

There you have it. That might have been a lot to take in, but no one ever said that navigating the world of finance was simple and easy. There are many nuances to financial management and responsibility. Hopefully, this book will have successfully exposed and acquainted you with those nuances. The goal is simple. It's to always put yourself in the best position to achieve your financial goals. This entails you having whatever tools and knowledge that is necessary to do exactly that.

In this book, we made a decision to address a problem: debt. However, we also realized that debt is just a manifestation of a lot of root problems and causes. This book shed some light onto how the accumulation of minor mistakes and poor financial habits may have led you to be caught in a debt problem. Then, you were also educated on what debt really is and how it wears many faces. There are many misconceptions surrounding debt, and these false mindsets can further aggravate a person's financial stature.

After that, you were equipped with all of the best practices and tips that you could incorporate into your own life. These tips weren't just designed to help get you out of debt. Additionally, they were designed to help keep you out of debt as well. The last thing that you would ever want once you get out of your debt is to fall back on your financially treacherous ways. On top of that, you were also given valuable education on how you can start to grow your wealth now that you're free from the chains of debt. After all, it's a constant uphill battle that never stops, even when you're no longer subject to the torment of creditors and lenders. Attaining financial independence and security has a lot to do with reinforcing good habits and staying disciplined. This book did its part by exposing you to all of the best practices. Now, you just have to do your part in making sure that you put your knowledge to good use.

If you ever feel like you don't have what it takes to get out of the hole and achieve financial security, get that thought out of your mind immediately. Remind yourself that so many people have been where you are now and managed to find success in their lives. In fact, so many people have probably had it much worse than you and were able to uplift themselves. At the end of the day, you can have all of the tools and knowledge that you could possibly need. However, if you don't believe in yourself, then you've already lost. Always maintain your confidence and you're going to turn out just fine.

References

Amadeo, K. (2019, May 30). Certificates of Deposit Explained With Pros and Cons. Retrieved from https://www.thebalance.com/certificates-of-deposit-3305913

Berger, R. (2016, March 23). 7 Budgeting Tools To Better Manage Your Money. Retrieved from https://www.forbes.com/sites/robertberger/2015/11/19/7-budgeting-tools-to-better-manage-your-money/#7a3c616f4274

Brannan, C. (2020, February 29). Good Debt Vs. Bad Debt. Retrieved from https://www.forbes.com/advisor/loans/good-debt-vs-bad-debt/

Brooks, D., & The New York Times. (2008, July 22). The Culture of Debt. Retrieved from https://www.nytimes.com/2008/07/22/opinion/22brooks.html

Business Insider. (2012, July 12). The Worldwide Debt Culture. Retrieved from https://www.businessinsider.com/the-worldwide-debt-culture-2012-7?international=true&r=US&IR=T

Credit.com. (2018, September 5). 20 ways to stay out of debt. Retrieved from https://clark.com/personal-finance-credit/ways-to-stay-out-of-debt/

Fay, B. (2017, July 28). Debt Myths - Common Debt, Credit and Bankruptcy Misconceptions. Retrieved from https://www.debt.org/advice/myths/

Fay, B. (2019a, April 2). Good Debt vs. Bad Debt - Types of Good and Bad Debts. Retrieved from https://www.debt.org/advice/good-vs-bad/

Fay, B. (2019b, April 2). Hospital and Surgery Costs – Paying for Medical Treatment. Retrieved from https://www.debt.org/medical/hospital-surgery-costs/

Irby, L. (2019a, June 25). Lower Your Debt With Credit Card Debt Settlement. Retrieved from https://www.thebalance.com/lower-your-debt-with-credit-card-debt-settlement-960608

Irby, L. (2019b, August 29). The Dangers of Credit Card Debt and How to Avoid Them. Retrieved from https://www.thebalance.com/dangers-of-credit-cards-960217

Jayakumar, A. (2019, August 14). What Is Debt Consolidation, and Should I Consolidate? Retrieved from https://www.nerdwallet.com/blog/finance/consolidate-debt/

Johnson, H. (2020, April 6). 11 Ways to Get Out of Debt Faster. Retrieved from https://www.thesimpledollar.com/credit/manage-debt/11-ways-to-get-out-of-debt-faster/

Lane, R. (2019, May 31). Is There a Statute of Limitations on Student Loans? Retrieved from

https://www.nerdwallet.com/blog/loans/student-loans/
statute-of-limitations-student-loans/

Law, L. (2020, February 20). 2020 Consumer Debt
Statistics. Retrieved from https://www.lexingtonlaw.com/
blog/loans/consumer-debt-statistics-2019.html

Leonhardt, M. (2018, December 10). Here's how long it
would take to pay off the average credit card balance in every
US state. Retrieved from https://www.cnbc.com/2018/12/
10/what-it-takes-to-pay-off-average-credit-card-balance-in-
every-state.html

Maddox, C. (2019, March 12). Change Your Habits, Stay
Out   Of   Debt.   Retrieved   from
https://www.moneyunder30.com/change-habits-stay-out-
of-debt

McGurran, B. (2020, April 7). How to Start Investing: A
Guide   for   Beginners.   Retrieved   from
https://www.nerdwallet.com/blog/investing/
how-to-start-investing/

Nerdwallet. (2019, December 19). The 7 Best Budget Apps
for 2020. Retrieved from https://www.nerdwallet.com/
blog/finance/budgeting-saving-tools/

Pritchard, J. (2020, April 5). Get out of the Debt Cycle.
Retrieved from https://www.thebalance.com/get-out-of-
the-debt-cycle-4054269

Ramsey, D. (2019, September 23). How to Get Out of Debt
With   the   Debt   Snowball   Plan.   Retrieved   from

https://www.daveramsey.com/blog/get-out-of-debt-with-the-debt-snowball-plan

STASH. (2020, April 17). How Do I Micro-Invest? Retrieved from https://learn.stashinvest.com/micro-investing

Stolba, S. L. (2020, March 9). Consumer Debt Study. Retrieved from https://www.experian.com/blogs/ask-experian/research/consumer-debt-study/

Szmigiera, M. (2019, October 10). Topic: Personal Debt in the U.S. Retrieved from https://www.statista.com/topics/1203/personal-debt/